The junior church programme with a difference!

Three + One

Festivals Two

Michael Forster

Kevin Mayhew

First published in 2001 by
KEVIN MAYHEW LTD
Buxhall
Stowmarket
Suffolk IP14 3BW

0 1 2 3 4 5 6 7 8 9

ISBN 1 84003 644 3
Catalogue No 1500390

Cover design by Jonathan Stroulger
Illustrated by Simon Smith
Edited and typeset by Elisabeth Bates
Printed in Great Britain

Contents

Foreword 5
Introduction 7
How to get the best from this book 9

Unit 1: Countdown to Harvest Festival

Overview of the unit 18
Week 1: The parable of the talents 19
Week 2: The parable of the sower 25
Week 3: The parable of the rich fool 31
Week 4: All-age worship 37

Unit 2: Countdown to Church Anniversary

Overview of the unit 42
Week 1: The parable of the prodigal son 43
Week 2: The parable of the unforgiving servant 49
Week 3: Jesus forgives Peter for letting him down 55
Week 4: All-age worship 61

Unit 3: Countdown to Remembrance Sunday

Overview of the unit 66
Week 1: Cain and Abel 67
Week 2: David and Abigail 73
Week 3: Jesus washes his disciples' feet 79
Week 4: All-age worship 85

This series of books is dedicated to the worshippers of all ages at my own church in Anstey, Leicestershire, with gratitude for their openness and enthusiasm in field-testing and developing this concept.

Special thanks are due to Laura Doody and Claire Pearson for their help with the proof-reading.

Foreword

Welcome to the Festivals edition of *Three + One*! This is designed to complement the standard volumes, which are intended for use throughout the year, with material specifically designed to focus upon Harvest Festival, Church Anniversary and Remembrance Sunday. Another volume provides for the main festivals, Christmas, Easter and Pentecost.

As you will know if you have used the standard volumes, the emphasis in this programme is placed upon building relationships, including the children in something they may come to value, telling the faith story in engaging ways, and letting the 'learning' be a spin-off benefit. I am convinced that that is a more effective way of working with children than focusing just on the imparting of knowledge.

As with the rest of the programme, the sessions in this book are arranged in sets of four: three 'Junior Church' sessions building into an all-age service on the fourth Sunday – which in this case will be one of the festivals – when the children's work will be celebrated and valued by the whole church fellowship, and the adults will have the opportunity to learn both from and with the children.

I hope and pray that these resources will open minds of all ages to the wonder of God's love and the joy of sharing it, rather than merely fill them up with doctrines and ethical propositions.

All that will follow. The first thing – and the prime thing – is to *relate*.

Enjoy the book. Enjoy one another. Oh, and enjoy God, of course!

MICHAEL FORSTER

Introduction

(Please read this – I think you're going to like it!)

This series of books arose out of a particular need. We were finding the usual age-based 'classes' difficult to sustain in our context, and mixed-age groups seemed the only option – but the cry went up, 'You can't teach five- and ten-year-olds in the same class' (I'll have more to say about the 'teaching' idea later).

At the same time, we wanted to include the children much more in the actual planning of our monthly all-age worship which, until then, tended to be a bit of a one-man show that was done *for* rather than *with* them. But just when do you gather increasingly busy and pressurised children together to plan services?

This is what we decided to do. We would take an overall theme that could be presented in three weekly stories, and the learning process would consist of fun activities: story-telling, art and craft, drama, music, some of which could then become the basis for the all-age service. But what if some children could only come for two of the weeks? Would they be left out? Clearly, each week's story, while relating to the three-week theme, would need to be able to stand alone.

Wouldn't it make the all-age worship terribly long and overladen with material? Probably, if *all* the previous three-weeks' work were used – so the Junior Church would choose just one of the three stories as the focus for the service, but let the worship leader put it into context with the help of the pictures, models, etc., that the children had made. That would enable most of the art and craftwork to be on display in the church, providing a visual background to the storytelling. And storytelling really is the basis of communicating our faith. Ask any of our Jewish cousins! Or ask Jesus!

So this material was written, and some of it has been used, and the basic idea and format have been tried and tested. One exciting result has been the releasing of some previously unrecognised creativity as children who had not been in the limelight before took the basic ideas and developed them in wonderfully imaginative ways. In the very first month of using this material, we discovered some real hidden treasure – and we did so in worship where we could properly celebrate and give thanks for it.

And that brings me to the most important thing we learned from this. Don't let the all-age worship become a talking shop! The discussion-type activities will quickly lose their appeal if that happens. We saw this coming in good time and proposed the setting up of a Worship and Mission Action Group (definitely *not* a committee) within the church to carry forward some of the ideas that come out of these sessions. Such a group must be a 'ginger group' rather than a management committee. They should not get bogged down in the minutiae of keeping new projects going, but simply research ideas and present possibilities to the relevant meetings (more than once if necessary!) to ensure that they are not simply lost in a sea of good intentions. If that were to happen – if the cards, etc., that the discussion groups produce were simply thrown away or filed and forgotten, we think it would not be long before the worship became stale: 'Oh, another of those silly discussions, again.' However, if the action group is set up, and enabled to work well, the all-age worship could become a real source of inspiration for the Church's mission – something through which the Holy Spirit might breathe renewal into the Church and the local community.

How to get the best from this book

The book is based on three 'units', each of which is a four-week cycle: three Junior Church sessions, and one all-age worship. Clearly, you will need to plan so that the 'fourth' Sunday in each unit falls on the relevant festival. You will also, of course, need to plan how this fits into the year as a whole. In field-testing this idea, we actually took a little time to plan the year's outline. After that, it was a very simple matter to follow the system through.

As with the other volumes in this series, each session divides into a number of activities, and a worksheet is also provided either to do in the session or as a take-home resource. There will almost certainly be too much here for the single session of perhaps 45 minutes that most Junior Churches have – so *don't think you have to use it all*. (Nothing destroys a good learning environment like trying to cram too much in!) Choose what you think best fits your group in each particular case, and perhaps have other items standing by in case you run out. Much, of course, will depend on the number of children you have. A small Junior Church could work all together, whereas a large one might start together for the storytelling and then break up into several multi-age groups, each focusing on a different activity – some children producing art and craft work, others doing drama, learning new songs, etc. The important thing to remember is that the all-age worship in Week 4 should be a celebration of whatever has been done – not a goal to be striven for and which becomes a blight on the sessions because the children are under pressure.

Most importantly of all, remember the central aims. The session should:

- be enjoyable for all concerned
- make all the children feel valued and cared about
- contribute to building relationships

If you do these things, then the 'teaching' will happen, because children are great learners if the environment is right. They'll virtually teach themselves!

Let's have a look at each of the elements that comprise the sessions.

Thinking about it

This is vital – the advance preparation need not be unduly time-consuming or tedious, but it will transform the actual session. In fact, we found that the preparation required in using this material was much less onerous than preparing traditional lessons.

- An advance meeting of key people would be a good idea, when you can take an overview of the unit and ensure that the necessary resources are available.
- Then each week look through the relevant session thoroughly and give some thought to which would be the most appropriate and helpful elements to concentrate on, in your situation.

- Prepare any resources: art/craft materials, visual aids, legitimate photocopies, etc., that you need. Try to anticipate the kinds of questions the children might ask – or that you could helpfully ask them.

What's the point?

It's helpful to have a specific point in mind that we wish to convey. This does not mean we can't find other things in the text, but one point retained is better than five confused or forgotten – and more likely to engage the children's attention, too! They have the rest of their lives to explore the countless layers of meaning, so don't let's spoil it by cramming them too full of rich food!

Now for the session itself.

Doing it

Prayer

An opening prayer is offered for those who wish to use it. However, we should be careful about stereotyping prayer too much as merely 'talking to God'. It might be worth thinking about encouraging children to think of prayer as consciously *being* with God – sometimes quietly, but also in the more active parts of life. So let God join in the activities, the fun, most of all in the growing relationships between staff, parents and children. In a different kind of way, the whole session is 'prayer' – and both kinds are important.

For this reason, the prayers are short and are all focused in such a way as to point the children to that greater reality.

From the known to the unknown

Jesus understood well the first principle of teaching: begin with what people know, and only then introduce the new. His most effective teaching, according to the Gospel records, was in parables. Often, he simply didn't mention scripture at all.

That is not an argument against biblical teaching – rather it is a plea to make it more effective. Children are wonderful at making connections – much better than we adults with our 'disciplined' (trammelled?) minds. So we begin by appealing to what they know, and *then* tell them the biblical story. With little or no prompting, they often will then grasp joyfully and spontaneously for themselves what we so often labour painfully and ineffectually to drill into them – and no one is more guilty of that than I am!

Tell the story

Storytelling is the basis of keeping the faith alive. Our Jewish forebears kept their children in the faith by telling and retelling vibrant stories, often around meal-tables, camp fires or in other informal settings, with plenty of song and laughter to help it along. So a child-friendly version of a Bible story is the mainstay of each week's material. It's a good idea to read it a few times in advance, so you are familiar and can half-tell, half-read it to the children with plenty of eye contact and other interaction. Or you can get them to tell it to each other by acting it out – see 'Drama', below. You may also find it useful to have some visual aids handy, or think of some questions you can ask, breaking off from the narrative whenever you choose to ask, 'How do you think God felt about that?' 'What d'you think happened then?' 'What would you have done about that?' etc. This will all help to maintain the children's interest – with a little imagination you can easily keep them enthralled!

Respond to the story

The children's response to the story now forms the basis of the rest of the session. It's important that they're encouraged to be spontaneous and really engage with the characters and the action. Here you will want to focus on the forms of response that are best suited to your situation, but the first one, 'Discussion', should never be missed out.

Discussion

Keep it lively, informal, chatty – and don't let any child feel silly or wrong, whatever they say or ask. The important thing is that they grow by being able to interact freely with the text. You may want to feed in some of their questions or reactions to the storytelling in the all-age worship. Most importantly, don't be anxious about this section – and don't let the discussion become either too long or too heavy! Just enjoy a bit of a chat with the children.

Song

Some songs are suggested. Either revisiting well-known ones or learning new ones can be fun, and perhaps sometimes the children can teach some of the new ones to the adults in the all-age worship. However, be careful not to let the Junior Church session degenerate into mere rehearsal. Let them have fun singing the songs, confident that even imperfectly sung they will still form acceptable worship. If some of the children have instruments, there's no reason why they couldn't be used at this time. All the songs recommended in these pages can be found in one or more of the following Kevin Mayhew publications (among others):

- *Kidsource*
- *The Source*
- *The Children's Hymn Book*
- *21st Century Folk Hymnal*

Art and craft

This will probably form quite a big part of the session: children of all ages and abilities can work together to produce models, drawings, paintings, etc. A few ideas are suggested, but they don't need to be limited. This was the area where we found children really showed their ingenuity and made immensely valuable contributions, producing and effecting ideas that would never have occurred to us!

Some of the art and craft work will feed into the all-age worship, and the items especially designed to do that are indicated with a tick. You may want to put less emphasis on this item if you're not planning on focusing on it in the service. What is important, in the 'ticked' activities, is that the children know *why* they are preparing these things – a few simple words of explanation will help them to relate it to the story they have heard and the point you were trying to make.

In terms of drawing and painting, the options are limited only by the size of the group and the children's imaginations! They could build up over the three weeks a complete 'strip cartoon' of the whole story, to be used in introducing the theme in all-age worship. The pictures could be on a continuous frieze, or on cardboard placards held on poles by the children, or separate pictures fixed around the walls before the service starts. Children could enter at different points as the story's told, holding their placard, or – well, you think of your own ideas – they'll probably be better than mine, anyway.

Drama

A dramatised version of the story is included. It can simply be used as a dramatised reading, with different children literally reading the parts, or it could be developed, if your group has a flair for it, into something much bigger. Adapt it freely to suit your group. If you need more parts, try splitting the narrator's part between several children, or add in one or two new characters. During the free discussion of the story things might emerge that it would be good to include in the dialogue. Feel free to photocopy these pages and make your own alterations if you wish. The drama can then either be used simply as a teaching aid or rehearsed and presented in the all-age worship. An added touch might be to use a domestic tape recorder to record it – then each child could take home a recording of a play with their own voice on it!

Worksheet

This is included for you to use as you see fit. You could have some of the children colour in the pictures and display them at the service, or you could let a group work through the sheet as part of the session; or it could simply be given to them as a take-home sheet to help them remember the session and/or to share with their families.

All-age worship

This is the culmination of the unit, but please don't allow preparation for it to dominate and spoil the sessions. It's not a performance, and no one will mind if what the children produce isn't beautifully polished – the main thing is that they should be seen to be enjoying it.

The services are designed to be truly 'all age', involving the whole congregation, and – most importantly – giving opportunities for interaction across the age groups. There are no 'children's talks', but rather all-age activities.

This approach needs to be reflected in the overall balance of the service, so that it is one in which all people can participate rather than a children's service with the adults as indulgent spectators.

Let's take a look at the various elements:

Songs

Naturally, there will be songs specifically chosen by the children, or at least with them in mind. But including some more 'adult' hymns not only shows respect to the older worshippers but also requires the children to sample a more varied diet and hopefully broaden their taste.

Welcome and statement of the theme

An example is given, but please feel free to use your own words and adapt it for your own circumstances. It's an important element in the service, for it introduces the chosen theme and sets it in the wider context. It is also a jolly good opportunity to point out some of the creative work the children have done, and have it suitably acknowledged by the congregation.

Prayers

Again, an opening prayer is offered, but it's not mandatory! Local worship leaders will probably want to do something more appropriate to the particular setting.

Word and action

The Bible story selected from one of the weeks 1-3 is not only read but reinforced with an all-age activity. The essential point is to make this at once meaningful and enjoyable. If people enjoy it, they're far more likely to enter into it. One important point, though: you know your own congregation best, and are in a position to ensure that people aren't treated insensitively. If you know that Mrs X doesn't like being in the limelight, then avoid drawing attention to her.

There is one very important general point, which we learned in the field testing. Where this part of the worship involves discussing ideas, don't let it become a mere talking shop! The discussion-type activities will quickly lose their appeal if that happens. We saw this coming in good time and proposed the setting up of a Worship and Mission Action Group (definitely *not* a committee) within the church to carry forward some of the ideas that come out of these sessions. Such a group must be a 'ginger group' rather than a management committee. They should not get bogged down in the minutiae of keeping new projects going, but simply research ideas and present possibilities to the relevant meetings (more than once if necessary!) to ensure that they are not simply lost in a sea of good intentions. If that were to happen – if the ideas that arose from this section were simply filed and forgotten – we think it would not be long before the worship became stale:

'Oh, another of those silly discussions, again'. However, if the action group is set up, and enabled to work well, the all-age worship could become a real source of inspiration for the church's mission – something through which the Holy Spirit might breathe renewal into the church and the local community.

Finally, watch the time. People will warm to the subject and be difficult to stop! You will also then be deluged with responses, many of them duplicated in different groups. Keep the discussion short and to the point, and move on.

Offertory prayer

All we do and give is a free response to what God does for and gives to us. The offertory prayer is a good opportunity to highlight that point. This helps to avoid religion becoming 'works centred' rather than being a free, joyful response to God's grace.

Reading

Because you're using imaginatively rewritten stories, it's very important to read from a standard Bible in the service, and this point should never be overlooked. Children – and especially the older ones and the young people – need to hear the Bible read and come to appreciate it for themselves.

Talk

It's marked 'optional', but it's actually quite an important part of the service. As with the Bible, the traditional sermon is too valuable (when done well) to throw away. In a service of this nature, a short talk helps develop and maintain the skills of listening and reasoning. Keep it short, though, or it will have the opposite effect! On the other hand, if the service is running over time, this is an element that could *occasionally* be omitted.

Notices and family news

All too often, notices are regarded as an intrusion, and ways are often found to 'get them out of the way'. But surely, this is the life of the church that is being shared here – and should it not be offered to God, along with the lives of his people? In the service order here, I've suggested putting the notices directly before the intercessions, so they can then feed into the prayers, thus integrating them more closely into the worship.

This is also a suitable time to do something else – the 'Family news'. People who have, for example, a birthday, or a wedding anniversary, or perhaps who are changing jobs, retiring or whatever, can share that with the congregation. A supply of cards can be kept in the church, with a suitably general message in them, to be handed out to people along with the good wishes and applause of the congregation. This is one slot we daren't leave out at Anstey, or we hear about it!

Intercessions

If Jesus was 'the man for others' it's hard to imagine worship that is genuinely Christian and doesn't include some sort of intercession for others. You will certainly want to include some of the children's own concerns that have emerged in the sessions in these prayers. You might also want to use some of the artwork to help the congregation focus on particular things. Whoever leads these, try to ensure that they are done thoughtfully, with a concern for the whole of God's creation, and not just Christians.

Closing prayer/benediction

Another element that should be kept short but meaningful! This is where the congregation are sent out into the world to live in some way the values and ideals they have expressed in their worship.

Now, go to it!

Most importantly of all – use the material imaginatively; make it work *for you*. It is your servant, not your director. What matters is that all involved enjoy the sessions, learn about valuing and being valued, build relationships with each other and with 'staff', and learn along the way.

That's how Jesus worked whenever he could. And it's not a bad example to follow!

Unit 1
Countdown to Harvest Festival

Overview of the unit

Theme: Sowing seeds and reaping crops

We take three key events:

Week 1: The parable of the talents

The parable of the talents challenges us to take the risk of failure and trust God for the harvest.

Week 2: The parable of the sower

Jesus uses an image familiar in his day to encourage us to trust in the freely scattered love of God.

Week 3: The parable of the rich fool

Jesus shows that God's gifts are given to us to share, not to hoard.

All-age worship

Here, you may choose to focus on any one of the three subthemes, but place it in the context of the overall story and theme: sowing seeds and reaping crops. So while the specific theme chosen will be emphasised in the choice of 'Word and action' material, some of the art and craft work the children have done in the other weeks will be used to decorate the church and set the context of the wider story.

Important note

✔ The ticked activities in Weeks 1-3 are intended as the link material for the 'Word and action' slot in the all-age worship. You will only need to do one of these in full – depending on which week's subtheme is going to be the main emphasis in the service.

Week 1: The parable of the talents

Thinking about it

What's the point?

Contrary to popular opinion, the third servant wasn't denounced for failure but for not trying. The point was that *he didn't trust his master enough* to take the risk. Talents are like seeds – they have to be 'sown' if they are to increase. The other two servants experienced a kind of harvest – but only because they put at risk the resources they had.

Doing it

Prayer

Loving God,
we're here to say thank you for all your great gifts to us.
Thank you especially for the friendship of each other –
help us to enjoy our time together
and to share your love as we do so. Amen.

From the known to the unknown

Have the children ever tried to do something that went wrong? (Perhaps you could share your own memory of a cake that flopped or a DIY project that failed?) It was probably a bit embarrassing at the time, but the world didn't end, did it? Jesus wanted to show that being willing to take that risk is important if we're going to make the most of the life God gives us.

Tell the story: Matthew 25:14-30

(See page 22 for a dramatised version of this story.)

You mean you didn't even try?

D'you know what a talent is – when people say, 'She's got a talent for singing'? I'm going to tell you how the word came to be used that way. It started with a story Jesus told, at a time when 'talent' meant a kind of money – like a pound in Britain, or a franc in France.

Bart was a rich man. He had a big business empire, selling everything from nails to nutcrackers, from feathers to furniture. Most things people wanted, Bart could provide – which was why he was rich.

Bart had to go away for a while, and thought it a good chance for some of his staff to show what they could do. So he called three of them to him. John was very bright, and could probably handle quite a big project. 'You can have five talents,' Bart told him.

'Five talents!' John exclaimed. 'That's a lifetime's wages, to me. And I know just what to do with it.'

Then Bart turned to Sarah. 'You can have two talents. With your imagination you should do well with that.'

Meanwhile, the third servant, Sam, was getting really worried. 'I don't want the responsibility,' he thought to himself. 'I'd rather stay as I am, thank you very much.'

'You can have one talent,' Bart said. 'I know you're not particularly energetic, but see what you can do with it.'

John wasted no time. He knew exactly where the opportunity lay. Bart's business sold most things people wanted, but John knew there were a lot of people who couldn't walk very well, or couldn't carry heavy things home. So he took on a team of people. 'Go out into the villages,' he said, 'and make a list of housebound people. Then you can visit them regularly, and do their shopping for them.'

Well, in no time at all, things were really buzzing. John had found a whole new group of people to sell to. And it gave the company a caring look, too, so other people who didn't need John's delivery service still shopped at Bart's because they liked to deal with a caring company.

Sarah had always wished she'd got a bit of money, because she wanted to invent something. Her mum, Mary, was getting old and her hands were weak. She'd always loved oranges, but now she couldn't enjoy them any more unless someone else peeled them for her – and always asking for help was embarrassing. Sarah knew there must be other people like her mum, and thought there must be a market for a really good orange peeler for people with weak hands. Well, this was her chance. She spent her two talents on developing her idea, taking each new version of the peeler home for her mother to try. After months of patient work, she'd got it right and Mary was back to enjoying her favourite fruit again. Sarah had just enough money left from her two talents to start production of her new orange peeler, and before she knew what was happening, John's sales team were coming in with orders for it from all the surrounding villages. Sarah had a winner on her hands.

And what of Sam – what was he doing with his one talent? 'Huh!' he thought. 'I don't want any part of this. I know what'll happen – it'll all go wrong and then I'll get the blame because I couldn't live up to Bart's high standards. Well, I'm not getting involved. I'll just keep the money safe.' So Sam dug a hole and put the money in it, to wait for Bart to come home.

'Well,' said Bart, 'What have you done with your talents?'

John beamed with pride. 'Here are your five talents – and five talents profit from my new scheme.'

'Wonderful!' Bart exclaimed. 'I'll make you a partner in my business! What about you, Sarah?'

Sarah was proud, too. 'Here are your two talents back,' she said, 'and two more – profits from my invention.'

'Great stuff!' Bart congratulated her. 'I'm making you a partner in my business, too.'

So what about Sam? Poor Sam! 'Well, it's like this,' he faltered. 'I, er, I knew what a great businessman you are – what high standards you set – and I didn't want to let you down. So I kept your money safe by burying it, and here's your one talent back.'

Bart was sad. 'Even if you failed,' he said, 'you could at least have tried. If nothing else, you could have put the money in the bank and got some interest. I'm really disappointed in you, Sam.'

Bart threw a party for John and Sarah, to celebrate their success. Poor Sam had nothing to celebrate, so he got left out. And that was a shame, because Bart wouldn't have punished him if he'd tried and failed. What hurt Bart was that Sam didn't trust him enough to take the risk.

Respond to the story

Discussion

How do the children think Sam felt when he realised what an opportunity he'd lost?

- Sad?
- Sorry?
- Did he wish he could turn the clock back and have the time again?

What has this to do with harvest?

- Was John's and Sarah's success a kind of 'harvest'?
- Can making use of our talents be seen as a kind of 'sowing of seeds'?
- Having talents and not using them – a bit like leaving seeds in the packet and expecting them to grow?

Song

One or more of the following songs might be used here and/or in the all-age worship:

If I were a butterfly
Let us talents and tongues employ
Take my hands, Lord
We eat the plants that grow from the seed

Art and craft

✔ Cut some cards roughly in the shape of seeds and large enough for a few words to be written on them. (See 'Word and action' in the all-age worship for how this would be used.) Take a box such as a shoe box and decorate it to make it look special. Write on the front or on the lid: *[Your Church]: Seeds for Sowing.*

Draw or paint a picture of three coins with their values engraved on them: '5 Talents', '2 Talents', '1 Talent'.

This is the key picture, but you might want to do others in addition to it, such as:

- The master handing out the money to his servants
- The servants handing over their profits to the master
- The third servant digging a hole in the ground

Drama: You mean you didn't even try?

Narrator D'you know what a talent is – like when people say, 'She's got a talent for singing'? I'm going to tell you how the word came to be used that way. It started with a story Jesus told, at a time when 'talent' meant a kind of money – like a pound in Britain, or a franc in France. Bart was a rich man. He had a big business empire, selling everything from nails to nutcrackers, from feathers to furniture. Most things people wanted, Bart could provide – which was why he was rich. Bart had to go away for a while, and thought it a good chance for some of his staff to show what they could do. So he called three of them to him.

Bart John: you're very bright, and could probably handle quite a big project. You can have five talents.

John Five talents! That's a lifetime's wages, to me. And I know just what to do with it.

Bart Sarah, you can have two talents. With your imagination you should do well with that.

Narrator The third servant, Sam, was getting really worried.

Sam I don't want the responsibility. I'd rather stay as I am, thank you very much.

Bart Sam, you can have one talent. I know you're not particularly energetic, but see what you can do with it.

Narrator John wasted no time. He knew exactly where the opportunity lay. Bart's business sold most things people wanted, but John knew there were a lot of people who couldn't walk very well, or couldn't carry heavy things home. So he took on a team of people.

John Go out into the villages, and make a list of housebound people. Then you can visit them regularly, and do their shopping for them.

Narrator Well, in no time at all, things were really buzzing. John had found a whole new group of people to sell to.

John And it gave the company a caring look, too, so other people who didn't need my delivery service still shopped at Bart's because they liked to deal with a caring company.

Narrator Sarah had always wished she'd got a bit of money, because she wanted to invent something.

Sarah My mum, Mary, was getting old and her hands were weak. She'd always loved oranges, but now she couldn't enjoy them any more unless someone else peeled them for her – and always asking for help was embarrassing. I knew there must be other people like Mum, and thought there must be a market for a really good orange peeler for people with weak hands.

Narrator Well, this was her chance. She spent her two talents on developing her idea, taking each new version of the peeler home for her mother to try. After months of patient work, she'd got it right and Mary was back to enjoying her favourite fruit again.

Sarah I had just enough money left from my two talents to start production, and before we knew what was happening, John's sales team were coming in with orders for it from all the surrounding villages.

Narrator So, Sarah had a winner on her hands. And what of Sam – what was he doing with his one talent?

Sam Huh! I don't want any part of this. I know what'll happen – it'll all go wrong and then I'll get the blame because I couldn't live up to Bart's high standards. Well, I'm not getting involved. I'll just keep the money safe.

Narrator So Sam dug a hole and buried the money, to wait for Bart to come home.

Bart Well, what have you done your talents?

John Here are your five talents – and five talents profit from my new scheme.

Bart Wonderful! I'll make you a partner in my business! What about you, Sarah?

Sarah Here are your two talents back, and two more – profits from my invention.

Bart Great stuff! I'm making you a partner in my business, too. What about you, Sam?

Sam Well, it's like this: I, er, I knew what a great businessman you are – what high standards you set – and I didn't want to let you down. So I kept your money safe by burying it, and here's your one talent back.

Bart That's really sad. Even if you failed, you could at least have tried. If nothing else, you could have put the money in the bank and got some interest. I'm really disappointed in you, Sam.

Narrator Bart threw a party for John and Sarah, to celebrate their success. Poor Sam had nothing to celebrate, so he got left out. And that was a shame, because Bart wouldn't have punished him if he'd tried and failed. What hurt Bart was that Sam didn't trust him enough to take the risk.

Can you tell from their faces which servant is Sam?

Enter into the joy of your Lord. (Matthew 25:23)

Sam's lost his spade.
Can you help him find it?

These pictures may look the same but can you spot 10 differences?

Start your sentence here...

T	B	E	S	E	R	T	V	M	W	I	T
A	L	K	X	E	R	M	J	D	E	Y	I
L	R	I	T	R	E	G	M	S	Q	D	U
E	O	L	J	E	S	D	C	H	E	G	R
N	E	C	M	R	N	U	S	D	H	R	F
T	R	F	E	Y	P	D	A	R	N	A	D
S	A	I	F	W	O	P	N	N	W	E	Y
X	H	E	T	M	U	R	D	S	A	B	E
D	B	M	Y	H	D	E	C	Y	S	D	R
R	H	T	M	E	T	B	A	W	R	N	Z
G	E	U	L	R	T	B	N	M	L	A	L
B	Q	E	N	Y	D	E	G	R	O	W	X

WORDSEARCH

What has this story to do with harvest?

Trace the sentence running through the grid to find out.

Week 2: The parable of the sower

Thinking about it

What's the point?

God is a recklessly generous giver: he doesn't 'target his resources', but scatters his love freely and generously, even in places we would think are hopeless.

Doing it

Prayer

Loving God,
thank you for being so generous with your love.
Help us to learn more of it in the sharing we do this morning.
Amen.

From the known to the unknown

Have the children ever tried to grow anything? How did they get on? Even if not, can they imagine the dangers a seed faces when it's growing – what with slugs and snails, extreme weather, etc.?

Tell the story: Luke 8:4-8

(See page 28 for a dramatised version of this story.)

Love is a seed to be sown

Jesus wanted to show how God loves us so much that he just scatters his love around everywhere – even in places where it seems hopeless. So he told a story a bit like this one.

Mike was a farmer and he was getting a hard time from Joe, his accountant, who thought he was a little bit reckless. 'You don't mean you sow *all* your seed in the ground?' he gasped in amazement. 'Don't you keep some in reserve, just in case?'

'Every single seed,' Mike assured him. 'And I get a good harvest every year.'

'Well, that's all very well,' said his accountant, 'but I hope you're careful where you scatter it.'

Mike's wife, Sally, thought that was hilarious. 'Careful? Him?' she laughed. 'You really ought to watch him sowing – it'd be an education for you.'

So it was that, when the sowing season came round again, Joe was there to watch Mike at work. At first, he thought Mike must have gone stark, staring bonkers. Mike came leaping out of the house, with a bag of seed over his shoulder, and started laughing and frolicking around like a child at play, instead of a serious businessman at his work!

'Isn't it a wonderful day!' shouted Mike as he pirouetted across the field. 'What a great time to scatter seed! What a great time to dance through the ploughed fields! What a good time to wave your arms about and shout for joy!'

Joe was horrified! 'Hey!' he yelled, 'mind the path – how d'you expect anything to grow there.'

Mike just turned a cartwheel and danced on, and as soon as he was a safe distance away, the birds came to the path for a free dinner. 'Well, that's a waste, for a start!' Joe exclaimed.

'Oh, I don't know,' said Sally, 'you're glad enough to have the birds around when they're eating the slugs and snails, so look on it as an investment.'

'Women!' Joe scoffed. Then he yelled, 'Look out, Mike – there's no point in sowing seeds among all those rocks – nothing can grow there!'

The thing that really irritated Joe was that Mike didn't seem to mind if some of his seed was wasted. He didn't seem at all concerned when seeds landed in the briar patch, among all the thistles and nettles – he just went on dancing around and scattering the seed as if it were some sort of a game.

'What you're watching,' said Sally, with a smile, 'is a creative genius who loves his work.'

'What I'm watching,' Joe corrected her, 'is an irresponsible juvenile, wasting valuable resources. I'm not at all sure I can continue to manage his affairs if he's going to behave like that.'

'Well,' Sally responded, 'he's been behaving like that ever since I've known him, and you've never complained about the results.'

Joe wasn't listening – he was watching in amazement as Mike stood up to his knees in a waterlogged part of the field and thrust both hands into his seed bag. Laughing merrily, he threw his arms wide and a shower of seed erupted all around him. Some landed in the puddles, some got into his hair or fell into his pockets – and quite a lot got carried away by the wind.

Mike was all smiles as he trudged back across the field. 'I love this job,' he said. 'All this seed, all this possibility – and I can just scatter it everywhere! Scatter, scatter, scatter!' And he laughed with sheer joy.

'Hmph!' Joe snorted. 'You'll be bankrupt in a year, just wait and see.'

Joe and Sally waited. And they saw. They saw the birds continue eating the seed on the paths; they noticed the seed that had landed on the rocks, growing and then dying for lack of water; they watched as the wheat in the briars got choked and died. And they watched as, all over the field, little green shoots appeared, grew, and turned into wonderful golden corn, waving joyfully at the sun.

After the harvest, they invited Joe back to check the accounts. 'I can't understand it,' Joe groaned. 'You just scattered that seed in that stupid, irresponsible way, and it's gone and produced a hundred times as much. What is it – some sort of magic?'

Mike and Sally roared with laughter. 'That isn't magic, Joe,' Sally told him. 'That's love!'

Respond to the story

Discussion

How do the children think Mike felt when he saw the seed he had scattered, growing?

- Pleased?
- Proud?

Song

One or more of the following songs might be used here and/or in the all-age worship:

Fishes of the ocean and birds of the air
Push, little seed
The word of the Lord is planted in my heart
We thank God for the harvest

Art and craft

✔ Make some paper 'seeds' – they don't need to be literally seed-shaped. (See 'Word and action' in the all-age worship for how this would be used.) The easiest way might be to fold a piece of A4 paper once down the centre, and then in half twice across, so that you end up with eight sections. On each one you can write a text that shows God's love. Write the texts on the paper and then photocopy onto card a number of times before cutting out the separate texts. You could also, if you have time, decorate some shoe boxes and label them 'God's seeds for sowing'. Some examples of appropriate texts might be:

✔ The Lord is slow to anger, and abounding in steadfast love (Numbers 14:18).

✔ The steadfast love of the Lord is from everlasting to everlasting (Psalm 103:17).

✔ The Lord watches over you (Psalm 121:5)

✔ You are precious in my eyes, and honoured, and I love you (Isaiah 43:4).

✔ For God so loved the world that he gave his only Son (John 3:16).

✔ The Father himself loves you (John 16:27).

✔ Therefore, there is now no condemnation for those who are in Christ Jesus (Romans 8:1).

✔ The love of God . . . be with you (2 Corinthians 13:14).

Draw or paint a picture of the sower sowing his seeds.

This is the key picture, but you might want to do others in addition to it, such as:

- thistles
- birds eating on the path
- rocky ground

Drama

See the next page for a dramatised version of the story.

Drama: Love is a seed to be sown

Narrator Jesus wanted to show how God loves us so much that he just scatters his love around everywhere – even in places where it seems hopeless. So he told a story a bit like this one. Mike was a farmer and he was getting a hard time from Joe, his accountant who thought he was a little bit reckless.

Joe You don't mean you sow *all* your seed in the ground? Don't you keep some in reserve, just in case?

Mike Every single seed. And I get a good harvest every year.

Joe Well, that's all very well, but I hope you're careful where you scatter it.

Narrator Mike's wife, Sally, thought that was hilarious.

Sally Careful? Him? You really ought to watch him sowing seeds – it'd be an education for you.

Narrator So it was that, when the sowing season came round again, Joe was there to watch Mike at work. At first, he thought Mike must have gone stark, staring bonkers. Mike came leaping out of the house, with a bag of seed over his shoulder, and started laughing and frolicking around like a child at play, instead of a serious businessman at his work!

Mike Isn't it a wonderful day!

Narrator Mike pirouetted across the field.

Mike What a great time to scatter seed! What a great time to dance through the ploughed fields! What a good time to wave your arms about and shout for joy!

Joe This is terrible! Hey, mind the path, Mike – how d'you expect anything to grow there?

Narrator Mike just turned a cartwheel and danced on, and as soon as he was a safe distance away, the birds came to the path for a free dinner.

Joe Well, that's a waste, for a start!

Sally Oh, I don't know – you're glad enough to have the birds around when they're eating the slugs and snails, so look on it as an investment.

Joe Women! [*Shouts*] Look out, Mike – there's no point in sowing seeds among all those rocks – nothing can grow there!

Narrator The thing that really irritated Joe was that Mike didn't seem to mind if some of his seed was wasted. He didn't seem at all concerned when seeds landed in the briar patch, among all the thistles and nettles – he just went on dancing around and scattering the seed as if it were some sort of a game.

Sally What you're watching is a creative genius who loves his work.

Joe What I'm watching is an irresponsible juvenile wasting valuable resources. I'm not at all sure I can continue to manage his affairs if he's going to behave like that.

Sally Well, he's been behaving like that ever since I've known him, and you've never complained about the results.

Narrator Joe wasn't listening – he was watching in amazement as Mike stood up to his knees in a waterlogged part of the field and thrust both hands into his seed bag. Laughing merrily, he threw his arms wide and a shower of seed erupted all around him. Some landed in the puddles, some got into his hair or fell into his pockets – and quite a lot got carried away by the wind. Mike was all smiles as he trudged back across the field.

Mike I love this job! All this seed, all this possibility – and I can just scatter it everywhere! Scatter, scatter, scatter!

Narrator Mike laughed with sheer joy, but Joe wasn't laughing.

Joe Hmph! You'll be bankrupt in a year, just wait and see.

Narrator Joe and Sally waited. And they saw. They saw the birds continue eating the seed on the paths; they noticed the seed that had landed on the rocks, growing and then dying for lack of water; they watched as the wheat in the briars got choked and died. And they watched as, all over the field, little green shoots appeared, grew, and turned into wonderful golden corn, waving joyfully at the sun. After the harvest, they invited Joe back to check the accounts.

Joe I can't understand it. You just scattered that seed in that stupid, irresponsible way, and it's gone and produced a hundred times as much. What is it – some sort of magic?

Sally That isn't magic, Joe. That's love!

Can you find the good things among the weeds?

WORDSEARCH

Find the following words in the grid:
SOWER, CROPS, PATHWAY, SCATTER, BIRDS, THISTLES, GROWING, DYING, LOVE OF GOD, GOOD SOIL.

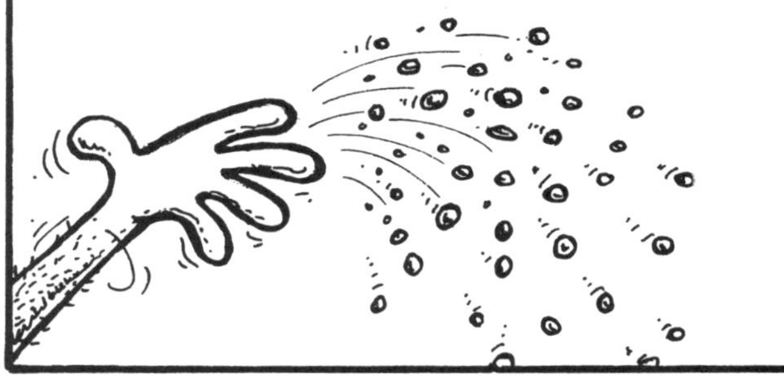

S	C	T	Y	A	W	H	T	A	P	G	C
H	T	H	I	S	S	L	E	S	S	R	S
G	N	I	Y	D	R	D	O	D	O	O	E
R	D	S	C	A	T	T	E	R	W	W	E
O	Y	T	R	O	W	I	C	E	E	I	T
W	I	L	O	V	O	F	R	E	S	N	S
I	N	E	P	A	S	H	O	E	R	G	L
N	R	S	L	D	I	S	P	D	X	R	E
T	H	I	R	T	L	E	S	S	E	E	S
T	H	I	S	T	L	O	O	D	S	O	I
X	B	D	N	L	I	O	S	D	O	O	G
L	O	V	E	O	F	G	O	D	H	Y	C

Week 3: The parable of the rich fool

Thinking about it

What's the point?

The trouble with the 'Charity begins at home' attitude is that all too often what it really means is 'Charity *ends* at home'! If we always put ourselves first, we may find that by the time we get round to thinking of others at all, it's too late.

Doing it

Prayer

Loving God,
thank you for being so kind and generous to us.
Thank you for the time we spend with each other –
please help us to enjoy it together. Amen.

From the known to the unknown

Have the children ever put something off until the last minute – and then found it was too late? Or have they perhaps always thought, 'One day . . .' but never got around to it? Jesus told a story about someone who never got around to it.

Tell the story: Luke 12:16-21

(See page 34 for a dramatised version of this story.)

For love or money

Ike was having a wonderful time. He'd got the builders in – and we're not talking minor house extensions here, either. The builders were building barns, for Ike's farm – the biggest barns you'd ever be likely to see. 'Get your backs into it!' Ike shouted at the workmen. 'I'll need all these barns ready in time for harvest. It's been a really good year, you know.' And he walked away, rubbing his hands and beaming to himself as he thought how rich he was going to become.

'I'll never need to work again,' he thought. 'This year's harvest will set me up for life.'

As he walked away, he met Eli, the local priest, coming to see him. 'I'm glad I've found you,' said Eli.

'Whatever you want, the answer's no,' grunted Ike. 'I haven't got time or money to waste on other people.'

'But you could spare a bit of land,' Eli insisted. 'That's all we need – just to make a little playground for the children to use. Wouldn't it be nice for you to have children playing nearby?'

'Look,' said Ike, 'why not come and see me again next year? It's not that I don't want to help, but I need to know I'm OK first. When I've made sure I've got no worries about myself, then I'll help you. But right now, I'm busy providing for my future.'

As Eli walked sadly away, Ike went home. 'I'd like to help,' he thought, 'but I just need to be sure I'll be all right. When I retire, with lots of time and money, then I'll be able to help others.'

Now, what Ike didn't know was that there wasn't going to be any future. If he'd known that, he might have acted differently – but of course, however rich you are, there are some things you just can't plan for.

Ike went home and made himself a bedtime drink. Children, playing near his fields – yes, that would be nice. Ike had been lonely all his life – well, when you're determined to make money, things like friends and family have to wait until later. 'Perhaps when the barns are built,' he thought, 'and all my crops are stored away, and I'm sure of a comfortable retirement – then I'll start making some friends. I'll have time for it, then.'

Just then, there was a knock on the door. It was Joanna, the woman who lived just down the road from Ike's farm. 'Hello,' she said, 'I'm sorry to bother you, but we're collecting for old Amos. You know he hasn't been well for a while, and now he needs some special treatment that costs a lot of money. Well, he's such a lovely old chap, isn't he, and everyone's given me something. Could you spare a couple of coins?'

Ike really wished this had happened later. In a couple of weeks he'd know the crops were safe, and he could give something then. But this was just too soon for him to take risks. 'I'm sorry,' he said, 'I'm saving for my retirement. Come back in a few months, and I'll know whether I can afford to give or not.'

Joanna looked shocked. 'If he doesn't get his treatment, Amos won't be here in a few months,' she said. 'Anyway, you must be able to afford something for a man like him – he's so well loved.'

Ike was getting angry – but only because he was feeling guilty. 'If he's so well loved,' he shouted, 'then I've no doubt you'll get enough from other people. I have to take care of myself, because I haven't got people who love me.'

'No, and I'm not surprised!' replied Joanna, angrily. 'I hope you have a long, lonely retirement, Ike.'

Well, the most amazing thing happened that night. Ike died. Just like that. No one knew why – perhaps he had a strange disease that didn't have any symptoms. Anyway, whatever it was, it put paid to his retirement plans. He died all alone. No one to hold his hand, or comfort him. And when the news got out, nobody cried.

Eli the priest did Ike's funeral, and he didn't expect any mourners to be there, because Ike had no friends. But there was just one. Old Amos struggled along to pay his respects. 'Poor Ike,' he said. 'I always felt sorry for him, all alone in that big house. And I'm so well off, with all the friends I've got.'

'Poor Ike' is right! All that wealth, and no one to love!

Respond to the story

Discussion

What sort of person do the children think Ike was?

- Was he a happy man?
- Might he have been lonely, perhaps?

In what ways could Ike have made himself happier?

- Building up friendships?
- Being interested in more things?

Song

One or more of the following songs might be used here and/or in the all-age worship:

Brother, sister, let me serve you
There are people who live in mansions
When God made the garden of creation
When your Father made the world
Who made the corn grow?

Art and craft

✔ Make a 'Round Tuit' – a cardboard disc with 'Round Tuit' written on the front in large letters, and some means of putting it on display, be it a hole in the top to hang it on a hook or a piece of 'Blu-Tack' on the back. (See 'Word and action' in the all-age worship for how this would be used.) Prepare a large piece of paper, such as a flip-chart sheet, with the heading 'When the time is right', and another piece of paper reading 'The time is now!' sized so as to fit over the original heading. Arrange for someone to be your helper, and go over what they will have to do in the service. Ask them to slip quietly out of the immediate worship area as you start the activity.

Draw or paint a picture of Ike watching his barns being built.

This is the key picture, but you might want to do others in addition to it, such as:

- Ike counting his money
- Eli and Ike arguing
- Ike's fields, full of golden corn

Drama

See the next page for a dramatised version of the story.

Drama: For love or money

Narrator Ike was having a wonderful time. He'd got the builders in – and we're not talking minor house extensions here, either. The builders were building barns, for Ike's farm – the biggest barns you'd ever be likely to see.

Ike Get your backs into it, you workmen. I'll need all these barns ready in time for harvest. It's been a really good year, you know.

Narrator Ike walked away, rubbing his hands and beaming to himself as he thought how rich he was going to become.

Ike I'll never need to work again. This year's harvest will set me up for life.

Narrator As he walked away, he met Eli, the local priest, coming to see him.

Eli I'm glad I've found you, Ike.

Ike Whatever you want, Eli, the answer's no. I haven't got time or money to waste on other people.

Eli But you could spare a bit of land. That's all we need – just to make a little playground for the children to use. Wouldn't it be nice for you to have children playing nearby?

Ike Look, why not come and see me again next year? It's not that I don't want to help, but I need to know I'm OK first. When I've made sure I've got no worries about myself, then I'll help you. But right now, I'm busy providing for my future.

Narrator As Eli walked sadly away, Ike went home.

Ike I'd like to help, but I just need to be sure I'll be all right. When I retire, with lots of time and money, then I'll be able to help others.

Narrator Now, what Ike didn't know was that there wasn't going to be any future. If he'd known that, he might have acted differently – but of course, however rich you are, there are some things you just can't plan for. Ike went home and made himself a bedtime drink.

Ike Children, playing near my fields – yes, that would be nice. I've had a pretty lonely life – well, when you're determined to make money, things like friends and family have to wait until later. Perhaps when the barns are built, and all my crops are stored away, and I'm sure of a comfortable retirement – then I'll start making some friends. I'll have time for it, then.

Narrator Just then, there was a knock on the door. It was Joanna, the woman who lived just down the road from Ike's farm.

Joanna Hello, I'm sorry to bother you, but we're collecting for old Amos. You know he hasn't been well for a while, and now he needs some special treatment that costs a lot of money. Well, he's such a lovely old chap, isn't he, and everyone's given me something. Could you spare a couple of coins?

Narrator Ike really wished this had happened later. In a couple of weeks he'd know the crops were safe, and he could give something then. But this was just too soon for him to take risks.

Ike I'm sorry, I'm saving for my retirement. Come back in a few months, and I'll know whether I can afford to give or not.

Joanna If he doesn't get his treatment, Amos won't be here in a few months. Anyway, you must be able to afford something for a man like him – he's so well loved.

Narrator Ike was getting angry – but only because he was feeling guilty.

Ike If he's so well loved, then I've no doubt you'll get enough from other people. I have to take care of myself, because I haven't got people who love me.

Joanna No, and I'm not surprised! I hope you have a long, lonely retirement, Ike.

Narrator Well, the most amazing thing happened that night. Ike died. Just like that. No one knew why – perhaps he had a strange disease that didn't have any symptoms. Anyway, whatever it was, it put paid to his retirement plans. He died all alone. No one to hold his hand, or comfort him. And when the news got out, nobody cried. Eli the priest did Ike's funeral.

Eli I didn't expect any mourners to be there, because Ike had no friends. But there was just one. Old Amos struggled along to pay his respects.

Amos Poor Ike! I always felt sorry for him, all alone in that big house. And I'm so well off, with all the friends I've got.

Narrator 'Poor Ike' is right! All that wealth, and no one to love!

Help Ike find a happy retirement. Which should he choose?

L	S	E	L	F	I	G	N	I	V	I	G
O	E	L	F	R	L	A	T	E	R	T	B
N	L	O	L	I	N	E	S	T	S	C	A
Y	L	O	N	E	L	I	N	E	S	S	R
X	P	I	E	N	D	S	V	I	N	E	N
G	S	P	E	D	E	R	T	H	G	L	S
N	O	D	A	S	A	H	E	N	E	F	E
I	W	E	R	H	G	R	I	O	S	I	L
P	I	A	V	I	D	W	E	W	S	S	F
A	N	T	E	P	O	D	U	N	E	H	I
E	D	H	S	S	U	O	R	E	N	E	G
R	H	O	A	R	D	I	N	G	Y	Z	H

WORDSEARCH

Find the following words in the grid:
HARVEST, BARNS, FRIENDSHIP, LONELINESS, SELFISH, GENEROUS, SOWING, REAPING, HOARDING, GIVING, HAPPY, SAD, LIFE, DEATH, NOW, LATER.

Week 4: All-age worship

Opening song

A song praising and celebrating the faithfulness of God

Welcome and statement of the theme

Get one or more of the children to point out or hold up the pictures as you sum up the story:

In Junior Church during the past few weeks, we've been preparing for this harvest festival. We've been thinking about different aspects of sowing seeds and reaping harvests. First, we took the parable of the talents, and saw how the talents God gives us are like seeds that can grow and produce harvests – but we have to trust God enough to take the risk of failure. Then we learned the parable of the sower, and saw it as a kind of picture of how God scatters his love freely in the world, even in places where it seems pointless to us. And last week, we read the parable of the rich fool – the farmer who hoarded all his crops instead of sharing them, and never lived to enjoy the old age he was saving for.

That's the general picture, but today we're going to concentrate on: [*Name the episode of your choice*]

Prayer

– use whichever is appropriate

Based on Week 1

Loving God,
at this harvest festival we thank you for giving us seeds to sow,
and for helping them to grow into crops that we can use.
We thank you for the literal harvest of food,
by which we and others are fed.
We thank you also for that even greater harvest of your kingdom:
for the skills and resources you give us to use to your glory.
Please forgive us for the times when we don't trust you enough to sow those seeds.
Help us to remember how great you are,
and to trust you for the harvest of our talents. Amen.

Based on Week 2

Loving God,
at this harvest festival we thank you for giving us seeds to sow,
and for helping them to grow into crops that we can use.
Thank you for scattering your love so generously in the world –
even in places where to us it might seem pointless.
Please forgive us when we make your love seem small,
loving only where we are likely to be loved in return.
Help us to love as you love –

to sow freely and generously,
and trust you for the harvest of joy and hope
that you long to produce. Amen.

Based on Week 3

Loving God,
at this harvest festival we thank you for giving us seeds to sow,
and for helping them to grow into crops that we can use.
Thank you also for the seeds of friendship
and hope that we can sow,
and please forgive us when they slip down our list of priorities
and get forgotten because we are too busy
providing for ourselves and our needs.
Open our eyes to those with whom we should be sharing your blessings,
and help us to share them now, while we have the opportunity. Amen.

Word and action

– use whichever is appropriate

From Week 1

Have the story read, in either narrative or dramatised form. Divide the congregation into groups, ensuring that each group has a number of 'seeds'. Their task is to identify what 'talents' God has given to this church, and ways that they may be sown. Emphasise that you're not about press-ganging people to volunteer for jobs, but thinking in more general terms about the resources the church has that could be 'sown' more liberally in the surrounding community and increase God's harvest.

If groups need help, you might have a few ideas up your sleeve. Is the church good at organising 'bun fights'? Does the building have useful features that the community could use better?

After a short time, call the groups back to order and ask people to share their ideas. Pass the shoe-box round to collect the 'seeds' which will be passed either to the action group (see Introduction if you don't know what this is) or to other appropriate groups in the church for feeding into the church's mission.

From Week 2

Tell the congregation that the children are going to sow some seeds. Then let the children run (or dance if they want to!) along the aisles scattering the 'seeds' they've made. They can also scatter them elsewhere in the church – in the pulpit, in the porch, etc. – but concentrate mainly on the seating areas. Tell people not to worry about the seeds that land in 'barren' areas – you've got plenty and to spare.

Ask whether everyone has got a seed. If they have, it must be because some who had more than one shared what they had with those who got missed – such is the random nature of the exercise. If they haven't, then ask if anyone's got more than one, and suggest that they share!

They can take the 'seed' home with them afterwards – it will be a useful reminder. For now, simply reflect that this shows us how God freely scatters his love, like seeds that will grow into a wonderful harvest. We know that some people experience that love more than others – so we've got enough to share, haven't we!

Now, read the story – either in narrative or dramatised form.

From Week 3

Introduce the activity by saying that this harvest festival we're thanking God for his good gifts, and thinking about how they can be used to make the world a better place for everybody. Draw attention to the flip-chart page, and 'brainstorm' with the congregation any ideas for ways that the church might help people in the community. This might be about providing for sick, housebound or disabled people; it might be about initiatives to help reduce crime; it might be simple things like coffee mornings, drop-ins, etc. Occasionally point out the heading, and say something like, 'Of course, this isn't for straight away, we'll do it when the time is right.'

After suitable time, make great play of ending the activity and moving the service on, which is the cue for your helper to enter and ask what the list is. You can answer, 'These are things the church is going to do when the time is right – when we get around to it.'

The helper can then say, 'I see. When you get around to it. Well, I've got one of those – a Round Tuit', and solemnly present you with it.

You could then introduce the story by saying it's about someone who could have done a lot of good, if only he'd got a 'Round Tuit'.

After the story has been read, either in narrative or dramatised form, stick the new heading, 'The time is now', over 'When the time is right'. It may be that you can't do all the things on the list straight away – and some may ultimately prove too ambitious altogether. But that doesn't stop you from making a start on at least considering the possibilities and doing something – sowing some seeds of justice and hope – and the time is now!

Song 2

Offering

This may include the offerings of produce or other gifts that can be used as 'seed' – good clothes for a hostel for the homeless, or basic provisions for a disaster appeal (be sure to check what's really wanted, first). It may be introduced as a token recognition that all our 'harvests' whether of crops, products, success, friendship or whatever, come from God and truly belong to him.

Offertory prayer

Thank you, loving God, for all your gifts.
Help us to recognise how, in sharing your gifts with others,

we sow seeds towards the great harvest of love,
justice and peace that is your kingdom.
May what we offer here, visible and invisible,
be used to that end.
Amen.

Song 3

Reading

Leviticus 19:9-10 read from a standard Bible. Introduce it with words such as: In the Old Testament law, God warns us not to be greedy with the harvest he has given.

Talk (optional)

If you feel it appropriate (and if time permits) you can point out the implication that the resources the earth gives are not the sole property of those who exploit them but are given for the benefit of the whole creation. Apart from providing for the poor, this text is also about not wringing every last drop of profit from the environment.

Notices and family news

Prayers of intercession

These could be led entirely by the minister or other adult(s), and/or could include some prayers written by the children themselves – or simply some points that they have raised in discussion.

Song 4

Closing prayer/benediction

Unit 2
Countdown to Church Anniversary

Overview of the unit

Theme: A forgiven and forgiving community

We take three key events:

Week 1: The parable of the prodigal son

Jesus tells the story of the son who got everything wrong, brought disaster on himself and was forgiven and restored by his father.

Week 2: The parable of the unforgiving servant

Jesus tells the story of the servant who, although forgiven much himself, was too mean to forgive his friend a little.

Week 3: Jesus forgives Peter for letting him down

After the resurrection, the risen Jesus forgives Peter who disowned him and left him to die alone.

All-age worship

Here, you may choose to focus on any one of the three subthemes, but place it in the context of the overall story and theme: a forgiven and forgiving community. So while the specific theme chosen will be emphasised in the choice of 'Word and action' material, some of the art and craft work the children have done in the other weeks will be used to decorate the church and set the context of the wider story.

Important note

✔ The ticked activities in Weeks 1-3 are intended as the link material for the 'Word and action' slot in the all-age worship. You will only need to do one of these in full – depending on which week's subtheme is going to be the main emphasis in the service.

Week 1: The parable of the prodigal son

Thinking about it

What's the point?

There are many points that could be made, but the focus for today is the main point of the parable: that God longs only to forgive all who turn to him – however badly we've let both him and ourselves down.

Doing it

Prayer

Holy God,
thank you so much for loving us as you do,
and for giving us time together.
Help us to share your love,
as we share in the story and activities today.
Amen.

From the known to the unknown

Have the children ever done something so silly they were afraid to admit it? All of us either have done or will do something like that. It feels awful, doesn't it – especially when we just know someone's going to say, 'I told you so', or 'It's your own fault'. We can be very glad that God's not like that.

Tell the story: Luke 15:11-32

(See page 46 for a dramatised version of this story.)

Don't miss the party

Jesus was in one of his story-telling moods. He'd just told a story about a woman who had a hundred one-pound coins, and lost one. She searched the whole house until she found it. Just before that, he'd also told almost exactly the same story, but about a shepherd who lost one of his hundred sheep and wouldn't give up searching until he'd saved it and brought it home. Then he went on to tell a story a little bit like this one.

There was once a rich farmer – we'll call him Tom – who had two sons. Two very different sons. One day, the younger one had something to say.

'Father,' he said, 'I have something to say.'

'Go on, Barney,' said his dad. (Did I tell you his name was Barney? Well, you know now, anyway.)

'Well,' Barney said, 'I know I'm going to get a share of your money when you die, but could I have it now? I mean, by the time you die I'll be old, like you are now, and I won't be able to enjoy it. Go on, Dad, please give it to me now.'

Tom wasn't happy about it. 'I'll bet he'll waste it,' he thought, 'but he's a big boy, now.' So Tom gave half his money to Barney, who jumped on a camel and disappeared in a cloud of dust.

Barney found himself in a country a long way away from home – a country full of exciting things – a country where you could dance all night, and where people were really, really friendly – as long as you had money. And Barney had money. A *lot* of money.

Not for long though. Not for long at all. Quite soon, Barney ran out of money and had to get a job. Well, it was either that or go home to his father. And he couldn't go home – not with his elder brother, Jake, just waiting to sneer at him. Jake wouldn't have done anything like this – Jake was a good boy, Jake was. Anyway, back to Barney. He got a job looking after pigs – the pay was nearly as bad as the smell, but beggars can't be choosers. Then Barney started thinking.

'Last week, I was having a party with a hundred people who pretended they were my friends, and now I'm up to my knees in pigswill,' he thought. 'Mind you, there's not much difference in some ways – except that the pigs have better manners. This is ridiculous – my father's farm workers are better off than I am. Well, that's it. I'm going home. I'll ask Dad for a job. On second thoughts, I'll grovel. *Then* I'll ask Dad for a job.'

Back home at the farm, Tom was looking out for Barney – just as he had been every day – and saw him coming from a long way off. 'He's here!' he shouted. 'Barney's home!' and he went running out to meet him. He didn't listen to Barney's grovelling – just threw his arms around him and hugged him. 'Never mind the past,' he said. 'You're home, and that's all that matters.' Then he called out to a farm-hand, 'Hey, Zebedee, go kill something – preferably something we can eat – we're going to have a party!'

Tom found some beautiful new clothes for Barney, and sent him off to get washed and changed before the party. Well, he had to – the state Barney was in no one would have wanted to dance with him. When the party began it was like nothing Barney had known before – much better than all the parties he'd had when he was busy wasting his dad's money. But there was one person who wasn't happy about it.

Barney's brother, Jake – remember Jake? – came in from working in the fields and asked what the party was about. When they told him he nearly hit the roof! 'I've been a really good son to you!' he roared at his father. 'And do I get a party? Not rotten likely. But this son of yours wastes everything and you do this for him.'

'You're my son,' Tom answered. 'You don't want for anything. But *your brother* who we thought was lost is now found. He could have been dead – now he's alive. Can't you celebrate that? Come and join the party.'

I won't tell you what Jake answered – but I don't think his dad was very proud of it. So the story ended, with poor, good, deserving Jake shutting himself out of the party because he couldn't stand the idea that someone who *wasn't* good was getting a bit of love.

Funny things, people!

Respond to the story

Discussion

How do the children think Barney felt when he realised he was going to have to go home and face his father?

- Embarrassed?
- Afraid?

Why do they think his older brother, Jake, was so angry when he found out Barney was having a party?

- Because it was the wrong night and he had to wash his hair?
- Because he would have to miss something good on the telly?
- Because he thought he deserved it more than Barney, and was jealous?
- Because he thought Barney ought to be punished, not rewarded?

Song

One or more of the following songs might be used here and/or in the all-age worship:

A new commandment
God forgave my sin in Jesus' name
I'm accepted, I'm forgiven
Oh once there was a father
Whatever you've done, I love you*

Art and craft

✔ Make a sign saying 'Forgiveness stinks!'. (See 'Word and action' in the all-age worship for how this would be used.) Explain the activity to the children and get a volunteer to play the part in the all-age worship, as described on page 62. The arrangements in the church could be as simple or elaborate as the resources available allow. You could simply have a chair facing the wall in an appropriate part of the church, or it could have a barrier round it so the volunteer can symbolically lock themselves in (or out according to your point of view).

Draw or paint a picture of Tom watching Barney go away.

This is the key picture, but you might want to do others in addition to it, such as:

- The prodigal's return
- Tom watching out from the rooftop
- The party, with Jake outside
- Oh, lots of things!!!

Drama

See the next page for a dramatised version of the story.

* A song written specifically for this parable, in *Wake up, world!* by Michael Forster and Christopher Tambling (Kevin Mayhew, 1993).

Drama: Don't miss the party

Narrator 1 Jesus was in one of his story-telling moods. He'd just told a story about a woman who had a hundred one-pound coins, and lost one.

Narrator 2 She searched the whole house until she found it.

Narrator 1 Just before that, he'd also told almost exactly the same story, but about a shepherd who lost one of his hundred sheep and wouldn't give up searching until he'd saved it and brought it home.

Narrator 2 Then he went on to tell a story a little bit like this one.

Narrator 1 There was once a rich farmer – we'll call him Tom – who had two sons.

Narrator 2 Two very different sons.

Narrator 1 One day, the younger one had something to say.

Barney Father, I have something to say.

Tom Go on, Barney.

Narrator 2 Did we tell you his name was Barney? Well, you know now, anyway.

Barney Well, I know I'm going to get a share of your money when you die, but could I have it now? I mean, by the time you die I'll be old, like you are now, and I won't be able to enjoy it. Go on, Dad, please give it to me now.

Tom [*Aside*] I'll bet he'll waste it, but he's a big boy, now.

Narrator 1 So Tom gave half his money to Barney, who jumped on a camel and disappeared in a cloud of dust.

Narrator 2 A big cloud of dust.

Narrator 1 Barney found himself in a country a long way away from home – a country full of exciting things – a country where you could dance all night, and where people were really, really friendly – as long as you had money.

Narrator 2 And Barney had money.

Narrator 1 A *lot* of money. Not for long though.

Narrator 2 Not for long at all.

Narrator 1 Before long, Barney ran out of money and had to get a job. Well, it was either that or go home to his father. And he couldn't go home.

Narrator 2 Not with his elder brother, Jake, just waiting to sneer at him. Jake wouldn't have done anything like this – Jake was a good boy, Jake was.

Narrator 1 Anyway, back to Barney. He got a job looking after pigs – the pay was nearly as bad as the smell, but beggars can't be choosers. Then Barney started thinking.

Barney Last night, I was having a party with a hundred people who pretended they were my friends, and now I'm up to my knees in pigswill. Mind you, there's not much difference in some ways – except that the pigs have better manners. This is ridiculous – my father's farm workers are better off than I am. Well, that's it. I'm going home. I'll ask Dad for a job. On second thoughts, I'll grovel. *Then* I'll ask Dad for a job.

Narrator 2 Back home at the farm, Tom was looking out for Barney – just as he had been every day – and saw him coming from a long way off.

Tom He's here! Barney's home!

Narrator 1 And he went running out to meet him. He didn't listen to Barney's grovelling – just threw his arms around him and hugged him.

Tom Never mind the past – you're home, and that's all that matters. [*Calls*] Hey, Zebedee, go kill something – preferably something we can eat – we're going to have a party!

Narrator 2 Tom found some beautiful new clothes for Barney, and sent him off to get washed and changed before the party. Well, he had to – the state Barney was in no one would have wanted to dance with him. When the party began it was like nothing Barney had known before – much better than all the parties he'd had when he was busy wasting his dad's money. But there was one person who wasn't happy about it.

Narrator 1 Barney's brother, Jake.

Narrator 2 Remember Jake?

Narrator 1 He wasn't happy about it.

Narrator 2 Jake came in from working in the fields and asked what the party was about. When they told him he nearly hit the roof!

Jake I've been a really good son to you! And do I get a party? Not rotten likely. But this son of yours wastes everything and you do this for him.

Tom You're my son. You don't want for anything. But *your brother* who we thought was lost is now found. He could have been dead – now he's alive. Can't you celebrate that? Come and join the party.

Narrator 1 I won't tell you what Jake answered – but I don't think his Dad was very proud of it.

Narrator 2 Not very proud of it.

Narrator 1 So the story ended, with poor, good, deserving Jake shutting himself out of the party because he couldn't stand the idea that someone who *wasn't* good was getting a bit of love. Funny things, people!

Narrator 2 Very funny things!

Help Barney find his way home.

Can you spot six differences between these two pictures?

P	R	O	D	I	G	A	E	T	H	E	R
O	F	O	U	N	D	S	T	Y	W	L	A
R	A	L	O	U	S	Y	A	S	A	E	T
G	T	S	O	R	Y	Y	R	U	S	B	H
I	H	B	O	R	T	H	B	O	T	H	E
V	E	R	R	O	D	I	E	L	I	R	R
P	R	O	D	I	G	A	L	A	D	A	D
I	S	T	S	O	R	R	E	E	X	T	E
G	C	H	D	R	Y	M	C	J	L	E	T
S	S	E	N	E	V	I	G	R	O	F	S
F	O	R	G	I	V	E	N	E	S	G	A
C	E	L	E	B	R	A	S	E	T	V	W

WORDSEARCH

Find the following words in the grid: FATHER, PRODIGAL, WASTED, SORRY, FORGIVENESS, LOST, FOUND, BROTHER, CELEBRATE, PIGS, JEALOUSY.

Week 2: The parable of the unforgiving servant

Thinking about it

What's the point?

We fall out over the silliest things! It's a good thing God's more forgiving than we are, because otherwise we'd be in real trouble . . .

Doing it

Prayer

Loving God,
thank you for the friendships we enjoy here.
Thank you for the sharing and the fun.
Help us to learn about you today,
and more about what you would like us to be.
Amen.

From the known to the unknown

Do the children know people (no names, please!) who are really exasperating because they never seem to learn? Perhaps they borrow without asking, or say unkind things, and then apologise, but do something very similar a little bit later? Yes, it's annoying, isn't it. But before we get too angry with them, let's remember that that's how we must all seem to God! And God goes on forgiving and forgiving . . .

Tell the story: Matthew 18:21-34

(See page 52 for a dramatised version of this story.)

Forgiven and unforgiving

'I'll kill him!' Peter was yelling. 'If Andrew criticises my fishing just once more . . . That's the sixth time he's done it today.'

'All I said,' Andrew protested, 'was that he couldn't fish for compliments.'

'That's it!' shouted Peter. 'That's seven times – and I reckon forgiving anybody seven times is enough, don't you, Jesus?'

'Not by a long chalk,' Jesus replied. 'In fact I'd say more like, oh, let's see, seventy times seven.'

Peter was amazed. 'Seventy times seven? Well, that's . . . that's . . . well, it's a lot, anyway.'

'Four hundred and ninety, actually,' Matthew replied. 'Trust me – I'm an accountant.'

Peter had a very quick answer ready for that, but Jesus interrupted. 'God's way of doing things is like this,' he said. 'There was once a great king – right? And he'd got this servant who owed him a lot of money.'

'How much money?' Matthew asked – we've got to get these details right, you know.'

'Oh, let's say ten grand,' Jesus answered.

'Ten grand!' Andrew whistled.

'About a quarter of a million crispy cod burgers, at today's prices,' Mary Magdalene chipped in, 'more if you have them without batter.'

Jesus looked patient. 'Do you want to hear this story or not?'

'Sorry, Jesus,' Peter apologised. 'I'm agog.'

'Exactly,' Andrew cut in. 'And gogs can't fish!'

'Are you going to listen?' said Jesus, quickly stepping in between Andrew and Peter, 'or shall I go down to the sea and talk to the waves, instead – they would. Now, if I have your attention, this slave – we'll call him Simon – he owed the king all this money and the king wanted it back.'

'I don't blame him,' said Matthew.

'With knobs on,' agreed Mary.

'So he called Simon,' Jesus went on, 'and said, "I want my money". Of course, he knew Simon hadn't even got the price of a pair of shoelaces, let alone ten grand. "Don't worry, Simon," he said. "You needn't pay." Then, just as Simon was breathing a big sigh of relief, he added, "I'll just sell you instead – and your wife and children, and your belongings."

'Well,' Jesus went on, 'Simon begged and he pleaded – you've never seen anything like it since that sending off at the Jerusalem sports stadium in last year's cup final, remember? Well, Simon grovelled, and he cried, and kissed the king's feet and said he would get the money somehow.'

'Yeah, yeah,' Matthew said, 'we've all heard that one before.'

Jesus glared. 'Are you telling this story, or am I? Anyway, the king was a kind old character, really, so he forgave him. "You needn't pay me," he said, "Just forget about it."

'I say,' said Andrew, 'What a nice king!'

'A very nice king,' agreed Mary.

'Don't get carried away,' grunted Matthew, 'it only happens in books.'

'I've not finished yet,' Jesus said. 'Simon went running off to tell his wife the good news, and on the way he met another servant who owed him the price of a bag of cod tails.'

'They're ten a penny,' Mary cut in.

''Well,' Jesus continued, 'you'd have thought it was millions, the way Simon grabbed him, and shook him, and demanded his money. Of course, the poor guy hadn't got it on him, so Simon had him put in prison and told them to keep him there until he paid everything.

'Of course, when the king found out, he was furious. "I let you off a debt of ten grand," he reminded Simon, "and now you've been and gone and done this – so into prison you go until you've paid the ten grand." And he had him thrown into the cell.'

'Too right!' said Andrew.

'Deserved all he got,' Peter added.

'Ungrateful little wretch!' hissed Mary Magdalene.

'Fine,' Jesus smiled. 'So does this mean I can expect you lot to be civil to one another from now on?'

Respond to the story

Discussion

In the story Jesus told, why do the children think Simon got so impatient?

- Because he was selfish?
- Because he'd already forgotten how much he'd been forgiven?
- Because he thought that having been forgiven made him better than other people?

What did Jesus' disciples learn from the story?

- That when we owe money we needn't pay?
- That God's just an old softie with no standards?
- That God loves us so much that he wants us to be his friends?
- That if we're God's friends, we should try to be more like him?

Song

One or more of the following songs might be used here and/or in the all-age worship:

Brother, sister, let me serve you
God forgave my sin
Hear what God says
Make me a channel of your peace

Art and craft

✔ Divide a piece of A4 paper into ten sections vertically and seven horizontally. You should end up with seventy 'cells' each about 3cm square. Photocopy this onto seven sheets of card – if you can find different colours of card it will make it more fun – and get the children to cut out the 490 pieces, storing them in a container ready for the service. (See 'Word and action' in the all-age worship for how this would be used.)

Draw or paint a picture of the servant in prison.

This is the key picture, but you might want to do others in addition to it, such as:

- The king pronouncing judgement
- The unforgiving servant attacking the other

Drama

See the next page for a dramatised version of the story.

Drama: Forgiven and unforgiving

Peter I'll kill him! If Andrew criticises my fishing just once more . . . That's the sixth time he's done it today.

Andrew All I said was that Peter couldn't fish for compliments.

Peter That's it! That's seven times – and I reckon forgiving anybody seven times is enough, don't you, Jesus?

Jesus Not by a long chalk. In fact I'd say more like, oh, let's see, seventy times seven.

Peter Seventy times seven? Well, that's . . . that's . . . well, it's a lot, anyway.

Matthew Four hundred and ninety, actually. Trust me – I'm an accountant.

Peter Yes, Matthew – and we all know about –

Jesus Listen to me. God's way of doing things is like this. There was once a great king – right? And he'd got this servant who owed him a lot of money.

Matthew How much money? We've got to get these details right, you know.

Jesus Oh, let's say ten grand.

Andrew Ten grand!

Mary About a quarter of a million crispy cod burgers, at beach market prices – more if you have them without batter.

Jesus Do you want to hear this story or not?

Peter Sorry, Jesus. I'm agog.

Andrew Exactly – and gogs can't fish!

Jesus Are you going to listen, or shall I go down to the sea and talk to the waves, instead – they would. Now, if I have your attention, this slave – we'll call him Simon – he owed the king all this money and the king wanted it back.

Matthew I don't blame him.

Mary With knobs on.

Jesus So he called Simon, and demanded his money.

King I want my money.

Jesus Of course, he knew Simon hadn't even got the price of a pair of shoelaces, let alone ten grand.

King Don't worry, Simon, You needn't pay. I'll just sell you instead – and your wife and children, and your belongings.

Jesus Well, Simon begged and he pleaded – you've never seen anything like it since that sending off at the Jerusalem sports stadium in last year's cup final, remember? Simon grovelled, and he cried, and kissed the king's feet and said he would get the money somehow.

Matthew Yeah, yeah, we've all heard that one before.

Jesus Are you telling this story, or am I? Anyway, the king was a kind old character, really, so he forgave him.

King You needn't pay me. Just forget about it.

Andrew I say, what a nice king!

Mary A very nice king.

Matthew Don't get carried away – it only happens in books.

Jesus I've not finished yet. Simon went running off to tell his wife the good news, and on the way he met another servant who owed him the price of a bag of cod tails.

Mary They're ten a penny.

Jesus Well, you'd have thought it was millions, the way Simon grabbed him, and shook him, and demanded his money. Of course, the poor guy hadn't got it on him, so Simon had him put in prison and told them to keep him there until he paid everything. As you'd expect, when the king found out, he was furious.

King I let you off a debt of ten grand and now you've been and gone and done this – so into prison you go until you've paid the ten grand.

Andrew Too right!

Peter Deserved all he got.

Mary Ungrateful little wretch!

Jesus Fine! So does this mean I can expect you lot to be civil to one another from now on?

Crack the code!

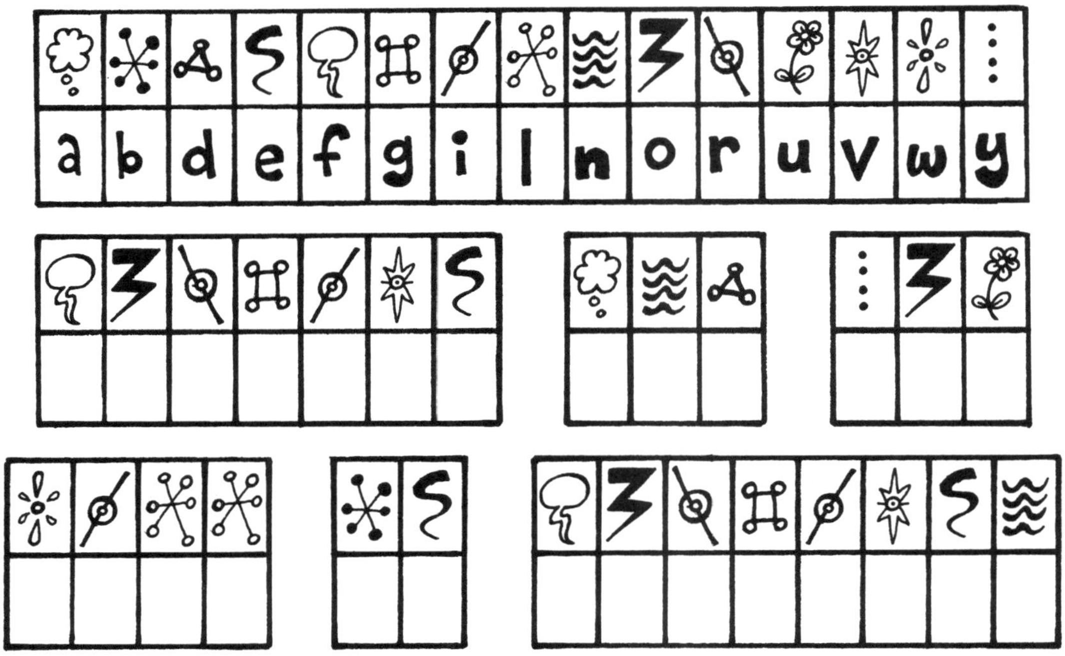

WORDSEARCH

Find the following words in the grid: FORGIVEN, UNGRATEFUL, SERVANT, KING, PRISON, SEVENTY, TIMES, SEVEN, DEBT, REPAY, UNPAYABLE, SOLD.

U	N	P	A	Y	A	B	L	E	D	E	B
S	E	M	I	T	Y	T	N	E	V	E	S
E	F	O	R	G	I	V	E	D	E	B	O
V	O	U	N	G	R	A	T	E	F	U	L
E	R	N	T	Y	D	D	E	N	T	O	D
N	G	R	O	T	E	S	E	V	E	G	E
O	I	X	K	S	B	V	E	B	T	O	R
L	V	I	H	K	I	N	T	O	T	Y	V
D	N	K	I	G	N	R	E	P	A	A	Y
G	F	O	R	G	I	V	P	E	N	P	N
S	O	O	L	D	T	N	A	V	R	E	S
C	F	O	R	G	J	T	A	P	E	R	B

Week 3: Jesus forgives Peter for letting him down

Thinking about it

What's the point?

Saying sorry and being forgiven isn't an easy way out. Being *truly* forgiven helps us face up to the hurt we've caused, and to our own weaknesses. Only then can the reconciliation really happen, and only then can we honestly move on.

Doing it

Prayer

Thank you, loving God,
for all the friendship we share.
Help us to be honest in our friendships,
and help us to know that you are part of them.
Bless us in all we do this morning, in Jesus' name.
Amen.

From the known to the unknown

Have the children ever said, 'Oh, that's all right, I don't mind', just to keep things sweet when really they were very unhappy? Or perhaps they've had it said to them when they've known the other person didn't mean it. Real friendship means we can be honest with one another and face up to the hurts. That's what Jesus did with Peter in this story.

Tell the story: John 21:9-23

(See page 58 for a dramatised version of this story.)

Forgiveness that hurts

Peter was feeling awkward. Only a few days ago, he'd been too frightened to admit he even knew Jesus – a real let-down, he'd turned out to be. Jesus' enemies were trying to kill him and they'd recognised Peter as one of Jesus' friends. Peter had done what – if we're honest – many of us might. 'What, me?' he'd said. 'I don't know the guy from Adam – whoever *he* might have been.'

But they wouldn't stop – just went on and on accusing Peter of being one of Jesus' friends. Three times he'd said he wasn't, before he was overcome by guilt and ran off. So they put Jesus to death, and Peter felt absolutely terrible.

By now, of course, it was much later. Jesus had risen from the dead, and his friends were all wonderfully happy – but Peter felt embarrassed every time they met. And now, Jesus was cooking them all breakfast – being really kind to them – almost as though nothing had happened.

As they were eating, Jesus seemed to sense that Peter was feeling awkward. 'Simon,' he said. 'Simon, son of John, do you love me?'

Peter was startled. Jesus hadn't called him Simon for ages. He'd renamed him Peter, which meant 'rock', but now for some reason he'd gone back to Simon. 'Well,' Peter thought, 'I've hardly been a rock over the last few days, so perhaps I deserve it. Yes, Jesus,' he said aloud. 'You know I love you – like my own brother, and then some.'

'Then you'll feed my lambs,' said Jesus. 'Won't you?'

Peter knew Jesus well enough to recognise the code: take care of my friends. Well, that was OK – it was the least he could do.

Then Jesus spoke again. 'Simon, son of John, d'you love me?'

'Of course I do, Jesus – you know that.'

'Then, take care of my sheep.'

The silence was heavy. Peter knew something was going on, but couldn't quite put his finger on it. Then Jesus spoke a third time. 'Simon, son of John, do you love me?'

Really, this was too much! 'That's three times he's asked that!' Peter thought, angrily, and he burst out, 'Look, Jesus, you know perfectly well that I love you – after all, you know everything.'

Then he realised. Indeed, Jesus *did* know everything! He knew that Peter had pretended not to know him when he was in trouble. Three times Peter had denied being his friend. So now that Jesus was risen from the dead, he was giving Peter three chances to say that he was. Trust Jesus to do it this way – make him face up to what he'd done, and give him the chance to put it right. Most people would either have held a grudge or just pretended it was all OK, but Jesus knew better. Then Peter realised Jesus was speaking again.

'Feed my sheep,' Jesus said. 'You're going to need to be strong, Peter. It was OK when you were young, and you'd fasten up your belt and go wherever you wanted. One day you'll be old – and someone else will take you where you don't want to go at all. Know what I mean?'

Peter understood – one day, his faith would really be tested, and Jesus didn't want him letting himself down again.

'That's for later,' Jesus smiled. 'What you have to do for now is stick with me. OK?'

Peter's faith grew and he became one of the greatest Christians. Not because he always got things right – but because he knew what it was to get things wrong – and most importantly he knew what it was to be forgiven.

Respond to the story

Discussion

How do the children think Peter felt when Jesus went back to calling him Simon?

- As if Jesus was trying to tell him something?

- As though he'd failed in some way?

How do they think Peter felt after the conversation was over?

- Glad it was all out in the open?
- Glad that Jesus had taken it seriously?

Song

One or more of the following songs might be used here and/or in the all-age worship:

Amazing grace
God forgave my sin
God never gives up
Step by step and on and on

Art and craft

✔ On a large piece of paper (at least flip-chart size) draw a cross. (See 'Word and action' in the all-age worship for how this would be used.) Then, on A4 paper write the following two sentences in large letters: 'SIN MATTERS THIS MUCH' and, 'I LOVE YOU THIS MUCH'. In order to make the lettering large enough, you might use two pieces of paper for each sentence. Photocopy them onto card, using two colours of card to distinguish the sentences, and then cut them up. Make enough copies for everyone in the congregation to be randomly given a card of one colour as they arrive.

Draw or paint a picture of Jesus talking to Peter beside the fire.

This is the key picture, but you might want to do others in addition to it, such as:

- The disciples eating breakfast on the beach
- Peter, in flashback, at the trial of Jesus

Drama

See the next page for a dramatised version of the story.

Drama: Forgiveness that hurts

Narrator 1 Peter was feeling awkward. Only a few days ago, he'd been too frightened to admit he even knew Jesus – a real let-down, he'd turned out to be. Jesus' enemies were trying to kill him and they'd recognised Peter as one of Jesus' friends. Peter had said what – if we're honest – many of us might.

Peter What, me? I don't know the guy from Adam – whoever *he* might have been.

Narrator 2 But they wouldn't stop – just went on and on accusing Peter of being one of Jesus' friends. Three times he'd said he wasn't, before he was overcome by guilt and ran off. So they put Jesus to death, and Peter felt absolutely terrible.

Narrator 1 Now, of course, it was much later. Jesus had risen from the dead, and his friends were all wonderfully happy – but Peter felt embarrassed every time they met. And now, Jesus was cooking them all breakfast – being really kind to them – almost as though nothing had happened.

Narrator 2 As they were eating, Jesus seemed to sense that Peter was feeling awkward.

Jesus Simon – Simon son of John – do you love me?

Narrator 1 Peter was startled. Jesus hadn't called him Simon for ages. He'd renamed him Peter, which meant 'rock', but now for some reason he'd gone back to Simon.

Peter [*Aside*] Well, I've hardly been a rock over the last few days, so perhaps I deserve it. [*To Jesus*] Yes, Jesus, you know I love you – like my own brother, and then some.

Jesus Then you'll feed my lambs, won't you?

Narrator 2 Peter knew Jesus well enough to recognise the code: take care of my friends. Well, that was OK – it was the least he could do.

Jesus Simon, son of John, d'you love me?

Peter Of course I do, Jesus – you know that.

Jesus Then, take care of my sheep.

Narrator 1 The silence was heavy. Peter knew something was going on, but couldn't quite put his finger on it.

Narrator 2 Then Jesus spoke a third time.

Jesus Simon, son of John, do you love me?

Narrator 1 Really, this was too much!

Peter [*Aside*] That's three times he's asked that! [*To Jesus, angrily*] Look, Jesus, you know perfectly well that I love you – after all you know everything.

Narrator 2 Then he realised. Indeed, Jesus *did* know everything! He knew that Peter had pretended not to know him when he was in trouble. Three times Peter had denied being his friend. So now that Jesus was risen from the dead, he was giving Peter three chances to say that he was.

Narrator 1 Trust Jesus to do it this way – make him face up to what he'd done, and give him the chance to put it right. Most people would either have held a grudge or just pretended it was all OK, but Jesus knew better. Then Peter realised Jesus was speaking again.

Jesus Feed my sheep, You're going to need to be strong, Peter. It was OK when you were young, and you'd fasten up your belt and go wherever you wanted. One day you'll be old – and someone else will take you where you don't want to go at all. Know what I mean?

Narrator 2 Peter understood – one day, his faith would really be tested, and Jesus didn't want him letting himself down again.

Jesus That's for later. What you have to do for now is stick with me. OK?

Narrator 1 Peter's faith grew and he became one of the greatest Christians. Not because he always got things right – but because he knew what it was to get things wrong.

Narrator 2 And most importantly he knew what it was to be forgiven.

Can you spot six differences between these two pictures?

Crack the Code: (a=26, z=1)

9,22,26,15 21,12,9,20,18,5,22,13,22,8,8 18,8 13,22,5,22,9 22,26,8,2

________ ______________________ ___ __________ ________

F	O	R	G	I	N	T	S	B	M	A	L
S	I	M	O	D	E	N	I	A	L	S	A
D	E	N	I	A	V	G	E	T	E	N	M
B	F	O	R	G	I	V	I	N	G	I	Z
P	E	T	E	S	G	I	A	D	E	Z	S
X	J	P	E	T	R	G	I	V	E	T	E
S	H	E	E	P	O	M	E	T	N	E	E
P	E	T	S	H	F	O	T	R	N	N	F
F	E	E	R	U	T	F	E	E	O	D	E
F	O	R	L	O	S	I	M	O	N	S	E
J	S	T	N	I	V	I	G	R	O	F	Z
F	O	L	L	O	W	Y	E	E	R	H	T

WORDSEARCH

Find the following words in the grid: FORGIVEN, FORGIVING, JESUS, SIMON, PETER, FEED, TEND, LAMBS, SHEEP, FOLLOW, THREE, DENIALS.

Now colour the squares containing FORGIVEN and FORGIVING in one colour to see what shape they form.

Week 4: All-age worship

Opening Song

A song praising and celebrating the faithfulness of God

Welcome and statement of the theme

Get one or more of the children to point out or hold up the pictures as you sum up the story:

Welcome to our Church Anniversary service, where we celebrate our life as a community of forgiven and forgiving people. In Junior Church during the past few weeks, we've been preparing for this by learning about how Jesus helped people understand forgiveness. First we looked at the parable he told about the lost son – sometimes called 'the parable of the waiting father', which is a better emphasis – how the son went away, wasted all his money and got himself into terrible difficulties, but when he went home his father threw a party and celebrated his return. Then we looked at another parable – the unforgiving servant who owed the king a fortune and the king cancelled the debt. Unfortunately, the servant had a funny way of showing his appreciation – he went and punished a colleague of his, who owed him just a tiny amount of money and when the king heard about it he was furious. And finally, we looked at Jesus forgiving Peter who'd done one of the worst things a good friend can do – pretended not to know Jesus when things got dangerous, and left him to die on his own. We saw Jesus being painfully honest with Peter, and yet showing he still trusted him.

That's the general picture, but today we're going to concentrate on: [*Name the story of your choice*]

Prayer

Loving God,
we're here on this anniversary Sunday to celebrate our life together –
a community both forgiven and forgiving.
Thank you for the constant love you show us
even when we don't deserve it.
Forgive us for the times when our community life doesn't reflect that,
and help us, as we look ahead to another year,
to let your love and your values show more clearly in our life together.
Through Jesus Christ our Lord. Amen

Word and action

– use whichever is appropriate

From Week 1

Have the story read in either dramatised or narrative form. Then begin to wax lyrical about how wonderfully loving the Father was, forgiving his younger son like that. The volunteer should then jump up and say something like, 'I hate this story – I don't want to be part of it', and go and sit on the special (as yet unmarked) seat. You can then express sadness, but explain to the congregation (tongue firmly in cheek, of course!) that this particular child has a real problem with the prodigal son getting away with it like that. The child thinks the father should have punished him, and it was really the older brother who was right. In fact, *this* is what they think (place the sign saying 'Forgiveness Stinks!' on the wall over the child). Now it's very sad – ask the congregation to chat among themselves for a bit and think of ways of enticing the child back into the congregation. After a few minutes get them to tell you their ideas. The problem is, of course, that whatever you do you won't really know whether they have come back willingly or because they have been pressured into it. No, the only thing to do is to let them come back in their own time. That, of course, is what the father did with the prodigal – and then he had to do it all over again with the older brother. The two weren't as different as Jake liked to think, were they!

Choose a really fun song for the next item, and let the volunteer 'decide' to come back and join the party – being, of course, warmly welcomed!

From Week 2

Have the story read in either dramatised or narrative form, and then ask the congregation if they can possibly imagine how much forgiveness that story represents.

Then let one or two of the children run down the aisles scattering the bits of coloured paper over the congregation.

Now, let's see how long it takes for the congregation to collect up those pieces and hand them back. If it looks like taking an inordinate amount of time – or if, as is almost inevitable, some pieces have got into places that are difficult to reach without undue disruption – then you can simply say that the point has been made. That is just one person's forgiveness potential – can they imagine that multiplied by the number in the congregation? If we could meet Jesus even half-way on this, there would be an awful lot of forgiveness in the air! The church would, quite literally, be littered with love!

From Week 3

Explain to the congregation that this is a great model of real forgiveness, as they're about to help you demonstrate. You're going to look at an important aspect of the cross. Explain that they have in their hands two vital and complementary statements the cross makes, but to discover what they are they're going to have to work together, They'll need to swap and compare cards (you might find it easier to assign one of the colours to each side of the church) until they have completed the sentences. When a group of people have worked out a sentence they can come and put it up on one side of the cross, using 'Blu-Tack'. When you have one of each sentence, stop the activity.

You can then point out that God's forgiveness is never an easy, 'That's all right, it doesn't matter'. God helps us to face the reality of our shortcomings while at the same time assuring us that he still loves us. So, to forgive as God forgives – to be a truly forgiven and forgiving community – takes honesty, and we find that hard. But if our 'happy fellowship' is to be genuine, this is what it takes. Jesus knew this, and Peter had to learn it.

Now, have the story read in either dramatised or narrative form.

Song 2

Offering

This may be introduced as our way of showing we want to be part of what God's about. We have received so much ourselves – forgiveness and other gifts, too – that we want to share it with others, and we symbolise that by our offering.

Offertory prayer

Heavenly Father,
we thank you for the greatness of your love,
which holds us together as a community of your people.
Accept the token we offer here,
as a sign of our desire to reflect your love
more and more in our life together. Amen.

Song 3

Reading

1 John 4:7-11 read from a standard Bible. Introduce it with words such as: The Bible reminds us that the basis of our faith is not firstly what we do but what God does. The love we show is part of our faith-response to God's grace.

Talk (optional)

If you feel it appropriate (and if time permits) you can point out that this is not 'cheap grace'. True forgiveness is hard for both sides, calling as it does for the real honesty which is only found where there is real love. You might like to sing the song, 'Let love be real', found in *21st Century Folk Hymnal; Hymns Old & New*, *Complete Anglican*; or *Hymns Old and New, Liturgical* (copies can be obtained from Kevin Mayhew Ltd.).

Prayers of intercession

These could be led entirely by the minister or other adult(s), and/or could include some prayers written by the children themselves – or simply some points that they have raised in discussion.

Song

Closing prayer/benediction

Unit 3
Countdown to Remembrance Sunday

Overview of the unit

Theme: Make peace their memorial

On Remembrance Day we honour those who have given their lives in war. The most genuine tribute we can pay them is to learn the lessons and make radical changes to our ways of relating so that their sacrifice will not have been in vain. Let's make peace their memorial.

We take three key events:

Week 1: Cain and Abel

Abel's gift is accepted by God, while Cain's is not. The Bible hints that the reason lies somewhere in Cain's hidden motives, but Cain is too humiliated to analyse that and simply lashes out.

Week 2: David and Abigail

David falls foul of the bad-tempered Nabal, but Abigail manages to make peace where the time-honoured responses threaten terrible bloodshed.

Week 3: Jesus washes his disciples' feet

Jesus, the 'Lord and master' humbles himself before his disciples in order to model for them the new way of relating that is to characterise those who are part of his new order. We've taken a long time to get the message, but with Christ it's never too late.

All-age worship

Here, you may choose to focus on any one of the three subthemes, but place it in the context of the overall story and theme: make peace. So while the specific theme chosen will be emphasised in the choice of 'Word and action' material, some of the art and craft work the children have done in the other weeks will be used to decorate the church and set the context of the wider story.

Important note

✔ The ticked activities in Weeks 1-3 are intended as the link material for the 'Word and action' slot in the all-age worship. You will only need to do one of these in full – depending on which week's subtheme is going to be the main emphasis in the service.

Week 1: Cain and Abel

Thinking about it

What's the point?

Cain interprets God's rejection of his gift as a rejection of himself, and takes out his wounded pride on his brother. Childish, of course, but not particularly unusual. Whether on an individual or a national scale, the result is often all too predictable.

Doing it

Prayer

Loving God,
thank you for loving us all as you do.
Help us to learn to care,
and to see each other as brothers and sisters in your love.
Amen.

From the known to the unknown

Have the children ever felt that something they'd done wasn't appreciated, and taken it personally? (We've all done it, and admitting that may well help them to face up to it in themselves.) Well, that's how Cain felt, although he took it a lot further than we are likely to.

Tell the story: Genesis 4:1-16

(See page 70 for a dramatised version of this story.)

I am my brother's *brother*

Adam and Eve (remember them – the first people God made?) – well, they had a couple of sons called Cain and Abel. Now, of course, all brothers and sisters quarrel occasionally, but with Cain and Abel it was a way of life. Whatever one of them said, the other would disagree just for the sake of it and before the next sparrow chirped there'd be tears and tantrums.

'I worry about those two,' said Eve. 'One day, one of them's going to draw blood.'

'Oh, I don't think so,' Adam answered. 'They've never been any good at art. But I'm very much afraid one of them might get hurt if they don't stop quarrelling.'

Before Eve could reply, there were raised voices on the terrace. 'You give me that back – it's mine.'

'You haven't played with it for ages.'

'Well, I want to now.'

'Well you can't, so there.'

Now, if you're hoping they'd grow out of this silliness, you've got another think coming. The words changed, but it was essentially the same argument.

'You've ruined my cabbage crop!' Cain roared at Abel. 'You and those lousy sheep of yours.'

'Well, where are they supposed to graze?' bellowed Abel. 'You've planted crops on every inch of land, you greedy parasite, and there's nothing left for me to use.'

'Don't call me a parasite.'

'I'll call you whatever I want.'

'No, you won't.'

'Yes, I will.'

And so it went on, until they'd completely forgotten what the real argument was about.

The day came when Abel – who, as you may have gathered, was a shepherd, decided to give God a present. 'The very best lamb I've got,' he said. 'Only that will be good enough for God.'

When Cain heard about it, he was hopping mad. 'Trying to get God on his side, is he?' he seethed. 'I'll show him what crawling's really about.' He gathered the best fruit and vegetables from his crops* – and took them to where Abel was praying. 'There you are, God!' he crowed. 'Better than a pathetic little lamb, eh? Just so that you know, I'm your man – I'm the one to back, around this joint. OK?'

God wasn't pleased. 'Is this what you think it's all about?' he demanded. 'Trying to get me on your side? Well, I'm happy with Abel's gift, thank you very much – *he's* being honest. And don't glower at me like that, either – I don't frighten that easily. Look, Cain, I'd get a grip on that temper if I were you, while you still can.'

'Yeah, yeah, I know,' sneered Cain and stormed off. Later, he said to Abel, 'Fancy a walk in the fields?'

Abel should have known better. He went off with Cain and guess what – next thing Abel knew, Cain had killed him. Cain's temper had finally got the better of him. As Cain was walking home, wondering what to say to Adam and Eve, he heard God's voice.

'Hi, Cain – where's Abel?'

'What am I,' Cain sulked, 'My brother's keeper?'

'I know what you've done,' God said. 'I can hear his very blood crying out from the ground for justice – the same ground you expect to give you crops to eat, now fouled with your own brother's blood. Well, that's the end of all that. You're a man on the run, now.'

'I can't run anywhere,' said Cain. 'Anyone who finds me will kill me.'

* Like what, for instance – can the children name some?

God sounded really stern, now. 'Oh, no, death's too easy a way out for you,' he said. 'I'll make sure you have to live with this for a long time. Now, go.'

So Cain ended up in the land of Nod. Oh, don't get me wrong – sleep wasn't part of the deal, not with Cain's conscience. Nod was the name of another country.

That's where Cain went, and that's where our story ends. Because no one has ever heard any more of either Cain or Nod since that time.

Respond to the story

Discussion

How do the children think Cain felt when God appreciated Abel's gift more?

- Angry?
- Frustrated?
- Jealous?

What should Cain have done about it?

- Congratulated Abel?
- Learned from the experience?

Song

One or more of the following songs might be used here and/or in the all-age worship:

God said, 'Cain, where is your brother?'*
Make me a channel of your peace
Some things make you angry
When I needed a neighbour

Art and craft

✔ Prepare a 'bran tub' for a lucky dip – perhaps several if the congregation is large. (See 'Word and action' in the all-age worship for how this would be used.) Plastic buckets full of sawdust are probably the simplest method – they need to be small enough and light enough for children to pass around the congregation. In the sawdust conceal a number of simple prizes, but also some booby prizes – things that no one is likely to want: an old bottle top, an empty aerosol, etc.

Draw or paint a picture of Cain attacking Abel.

This is the key picture, but you might want to do others in addition to it, such as:

- Abel offering his lamb to God
- Cain pushing his barrow of food

Drama

See the next page for a dramatised version of the story.

* Written specially for this passage, this song can be found in *Wake up, world!* (Kevin Mayhew, 1993)

Drama: I am my brother's *brother*

Narrator Adam and Eve (remember them – the first people God made?) – well, they had a couple of sons called Cain and Abel. Now, of course, all brothers and sisters quarrel occasionally, but with Cain and Abel it was a way of life. Whatever one of them said, the other would disagree just for the sake of it and before the next sparrow chirped there'd be tears and tantrums.

Eve You know, Adam, I worry about those two. One day, one of them's going to draw blood.

Adam Oh, I don't think so, Eve. They've never been any good at art. But I'm very much afraid one of them might get hurt if they don't stop quarrelling.

Abel You give me that back – it's mine.

Cain You haven't played with it for ages.

Abel Well, I want to now.

Cain Well you can't, so there.

Narrator Now, if you're hoping they'd grow out of this silliness, you've got another think coming. The words changed, but it was essentially the same argument.

Cain Abel, you've ruined my cabbage crop – you and those lousy sheep of yours.

Abel Well, where are they supposed to graze? You've planted crops on every inch of land, you greedy parasite, and there's nothing left for me to use.

Cain Don't call me a parasite.

Abel I'll call you whatever I want.

Cain No, you won't.

Abel Yes, I will.

Narrator And so it went on, until they'd completely forgotten what the real argument was about. The day came when Abel – who, as you may have gathered, was a shepherd, decided to give God a present.

Abel The very best lamb I've got. Only that will be good enough for God.

Narrator When Cain heard about it, he was hopping mad.

Cain Trying to get God on his side, is he? I'll show him what crawling's really about.

Narrator Cain gathered the best fruit and vegetables from his crops* – and took them to where Abel was praying.

* Like what, for instance – can the children name some?

Cain There you are, God! Better than a pathetic little lamb, eh? Just so that you know, I'm your man – I'm the one to back, around this joint. OK?

Abel God wasn't pleased.

God Is this what you think it's all about? Trying to get me on your side? Well, I'm happy with Abel's gift, thank you very much – *he's* being honest. And don't glower at me like that, either – I don't frighten that easily. Look, Cain, I'd get a grip on that temper if I were you, while you still can.

Cain Yeah, yeah, I know.

Narrator Cain stormed off for a good sulk, and hatched a horrible plot.

Cain Hey, Abel, fancy a walk in the fields?

Narrator Abel should have known better. He went off with Cain and guess what – next thing Abel knew, Cain had killed him. Cain's temper had finally got the better of him. As Cain was walking home, wondering what to say to Adam and Eve, he heard God's voice.

God Hi, Cain – where's Abel?

Cain What am I – my brother's keeper?

God I know what you've done. I can hear his very blood crying out from the ground for justice – the same ground you expect to give you crops to eat, now fouled with your own brother's blood. Well, that's the end of all that. You're a man on the run, now.

Cain I can't run anywhere – anyone who finds me will kill me.

God Oh, no – death's too easy a way out for you. I'll make sure you have to live with this for a long time. Now, go.

Narrator So Cain ended up in the land of Nod. Oh, don't get me wrong – sleep wasn't part of the deal, not with Cain's conscience. Nod was the name of another country. That's where Cain went, and that's where our story ends. Because no one has ever heard any more of either Cain or Nod since that time.

Am I my brother's keeper?

Crack the code for an answer

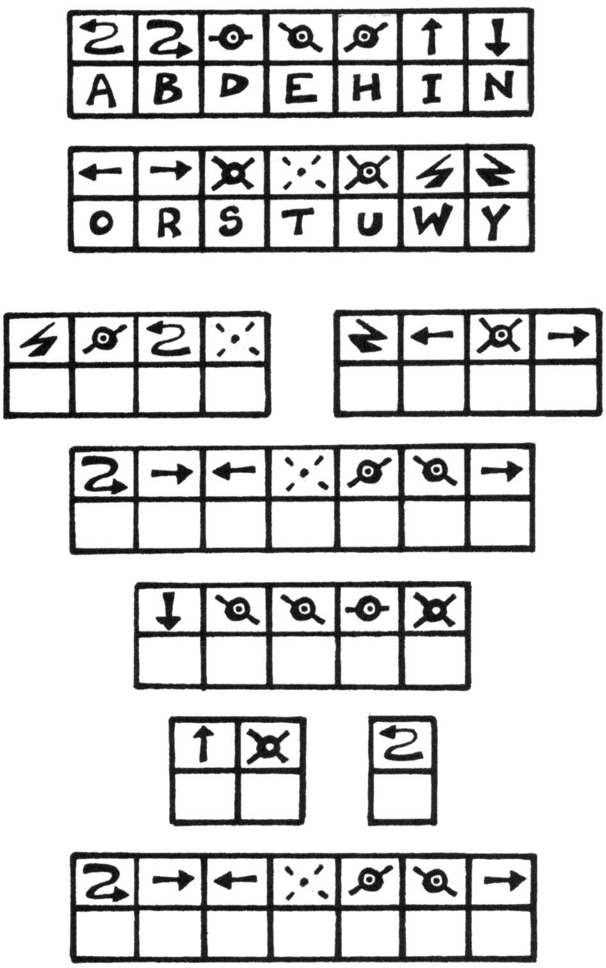

WORDSEARCH

Find the following words in the grid:
CAIN, ABEL, ADAM, EVE, CROPS,
LAMB, KEEPER, BROTHER,
FUGITIVE, CONSCIENCE.

C	A	I	R	E	H	T	O	R	B	N	A
C	O	N	S	C	I	E	N	C	E	D	B
R	A	F	U	G	I	T	I	V	A	B	E
O	N	I	E	N	C	E	I	M	B	X	G
P	C	A	N	A	D	A	E	L	E	B	A
S	C	O	N	S	C	I	V	R	O	P	S
E	I	C	S	N	O	C	I	L	A	M	R
E	K	E	E	P	E	R	T	A	D	A	O
P	A	M	B	F	U	G	I	B	I	V	P
E	S	B	E	E	P	E	G	A	M	B	S
R	E	V	E	E	V	T	U	E	B	A	I
C	O	N	S	C	I	E	F	A	D	A	L

Week 2: David and Abigail

Thinking about it

What's the point?

So many terrible conflicts have happened only because no one had the moral courage to back down or apologise. Pride, stubbornness and sheer, blind stupidity can too often govern a nation's, as well as an individual's responses. If we can learn while still young to recognise the signs and talk our way out of trouble, the world might eventually be a much better place.

Doing it

Prayer

Loving God, thank you for all our friends,
especially the ones we share with today.
Help us to recognise our own friendships
as signs of your love for all people. Amen.

From the known to the unknown

Have the children ever been caught in a confrontation where neither party wants to lose face? We all know the feelings that arouses, and how much easier it is sometimes to fight, rather than lose face – even if we know we'll get marmalised!

Tell the story: 1 Samuel 25:1-35

(See page 76 for a dramatised version of this story.)

Brains before brawn

Nabal was one of those guys you just can't please. You know the sort of thing – if you help them you're interfering and if you don't you've got no consideration. In short, he was a grouch. And that's not surprising because that's what his name – Nabal – actually meant.

Now, don't ask me how, but he'd somehow got married to the sweetest, cleverest, most beautiful woman you could ever imagine. Abigail, her name was, and she had a brain to match her beauty – which was a good thing because as far as anyone could tell, Nabal didn't have a brain at all. No one actually knew whether he'd never had one, or whether he'd lost it in a card game, but there was certainly no sign of it now – as became even more obvious when he came in from the farm one day, moaning and stamping his feet. 'That David,' he said, 'he only had the front to ask me to give him and his gang some food. Does he think I'm made of money?'

'I hope you weren't rude to him,' Abigail said, 'because I hear he's got a quick temper – and a lot of friends.'

'Rude? Me?' replied Nabal. 'Not at all – I just sent him a message saying he wouldn't get any food from me until he'd boiled his own head in a garlic sauce.'

Abigail was hopping mad. 'You said what? I hope you were joking. More to the point, I hope *he knows* you were joking.'

Nabal wasn't joking – you need wits to be witty. 'Load of scroungers,' he said, 'no homes, no jobs, on the run from the king – just because King Saul's gone mad and started killing everyone who disagrees with him is no reason to run away. As far as I'm concerned, David's bad news.'

'Oh, yes, of course,' answered Abigail. 'Really bad news, when he and his friends have helped with the harvest, guarded your sheep and kept poachers away from your land – yes, I can see how you don't want anything like that happening, you brain-dead son of an intellectually challenged earthworm.'

Meanwhile, back at his camp, David was just receiving Nabal's message. 'Right, men,' he shouted. 'The first four hundred to get their swords on, come with me – the rest can guard the camp. We're finally going to find out where Nabal's brain is – we're going to take him apart and look for it.'

Well, everybody hated Nabal, so in no time at all David and four hundred friends were riding out of the camp towards Nabal's house.

Of course, Abigail soon heard about it and started giving orders to her servants. 'Get me some donkeys,' she said. 'No, not Nabal – some intelligent ones. And lots of presents – wine, figs, bread, meat, grain – as much as you can find. It's time for some serious peace-making.'

Very soon, Abigail was riding out to meet David. Just imagine it: four hundred and one men, with sharp swords, long spears and fierce tempers, against one woman with a load of groceries. Hardly seems promising, does it?

When Abigail saw David and his men coming, she stopped and dismounted, and put on her sweetest smile. Now, that would have stopped a cruise missile in full flight, so David had no chance. He stopped, and Abigail turned on the charm.

'Oh, sir, I'm really sorry about that dreadful husband of mine. Of course, if he was bright and handsome and thoughtful like you, he'd never have said those things. Can you ever forgive us?'

'Of course I forgive you,' David beamed at her. 'Thank God I met you before I got to Nabal, because, believe me, there'd have been some blood flowing – and all over one bad-tempered old grouch.'

'Well,' Abigail smiled, sweetly, 'one thing you can say about my husband – he always lives down to his name. Now, I've got to get back before he picks a fight with his own shadow – and loses. Enjoy the food and the wine.'

When Abigail got back, Nabal was all geared up for action, standing at the gate with three farmhands armed with pitchforks, like some former-day Dad's Army. 'It's all right,' Abigail told them. 'The battle's over. Everybody won.'

Respond to the story

Discussion

Why couldn't Nabal have apologised to David?

- Because he thought it would make him look weak?
- Because he was a silly, proud person?

What would have happened to Nabal if Abigail hadn't stopped David?

- Well, it's obvious, isn't it . . .

Was David's reaction to Nabal's churlishness reasonable?

Who was the truly strong character in this story?

- The donkey who carried all the gifts?
- Abigail?

Song

One or more of the following songs might be used here and/or in the all-age worship:

Make me a channel of your peace
Peace, perfect peace
Shalom, my friends
When God made the garden of creation
When I needed a neighbour

Art and craft

✔ Using single sheets of newspaper, *lightly* rolled and fastened with tape, make some simple 'coshes'. (See 'Word and action' in the all-age worship for how these would be used.) Explain to the children as you do it that you are making these horrible things in order to help the church think about how dreadful war is. Ideally, you would make enough for everyone in the congregation to have one, but don't worry about it if that would be too time consuming. As long as there are a few symbolic ones around, the rest of the congregation can improvise.

Draw or paint a picture of Abigail talking to David.

This is the key picture, but you might want to do others in addition to it, such as:

- Nabal sulking
- Nabal guarding his home

Drama

See the next page for a dramatised version of the story.

Drama: Brains before brawn

Narrator Nabal was one of those guys you just can't please. You know the sort of thing – if you help them you're interfering and if you don't you've got no consideration. In short, he was a grouch. And that's not surprising because that's what his name – Nabal – actually meant. Now, don't ask me how, but he'd somehow got married to the sweetest, cleverest, most beautiful woman you could ever imagine. Abigail, her name was, and she had a brain to match her beauty – which was a good thing because as far as anyone could tell, Nabal didn't have a brain at all. No one actually knew whether he'd never had one, or whether he'd lost it in a card game, but there was certainly no sign of it now – as became even more obvious when he came in from the farm one day, moaning and stamping his feet.

Nabal That David! He only had the front to ask me to give him and his gang some food. Does he think I'm made of money?

Abigail I hope you weren't rude to him, because I hear he's got a quick temper – and a lot of friends.

Nabal Rude? Me? Not at all – I just sent him a message saying he wouldn't get any food from me until he'd boiled his own head in a garlic sauce.

Abigail [*Angrily*] You said what? I hope you were joking. More to the point, I hope *he knew* you were joking.

Narrator Nabal wasn't joking – you need wits to be witty.

Nabal Load of scroungers – no homes, no jobs, on the run from the king – just because King Saul's gone mad and started killing everyone who disagrees with him is no reason to run away. As far as I'm concerned, David's bad news.

Abigail Oh, yes, of course! Really bad news, when he and his friends have helped with the harvest, guarded your sheep and kept poachers away from your land – yes, I can see how you don't want anything like that happening, you brain-dead son of an intellectually challenged earthworm.

Narrator Meanwhile, back at his camp, David was just receiving Nabal's message.

David Right, men, the first four hundred to get their swords on, come with me – the rest can guard the camp. We're finally going to find out where Nabal's brain is – we're going to take him apart and look for it.

Narrator Well, everybody hated Nabal, so in no time at all David and four hundred friends were riding out of the camp towards Nabal's house. Luckily, Abigail got wind of it and started giving orders to her servants.

Abigail Get me some donkeys. No, not Nabal – some intelligent ones. And lots of presents – wine, figs, bread, meat, grain – as much as you can find. It's time for some serious peace-making.

Narrator Very soon, Abigail was riding out to meet David. Just imagine it: four hundred and one men, with sharp swords, long spears and fierce tempers, against one woman with a load of groceries. Hardly seems promising, does it? When Abigail saw David and his men coming, she stopped and dismounted, and put on her sweetest smile. Now, that would have stopped a cruise missile in full flight, so David had no chance. He stopped, and Abigail turned on the charm.

Abigail Oh, sir, I'm really sorry about that dreadful husband of mine. Of course, if he was bright and handsome and thoughtful like you, he'd never have said those things. Can you ever forgive us?

David Of course I forgive you. Thank God I met you before I got to Nabal, because, believe me, there'd have been some blood flowing – and all over one bad-tempered old grouch.

Abigail Well, one thing you can say about my husband – he always lives down to his name. Now, I've got to get back before he picks a fight with his own shadow – and loses. Enjoy the food and the wine.

Narrator When Abigail got back, Nabal was all geared up for action, standing at the gate with three farmhands armed with pitch-forks, like some former-day Dad's Army.

Abigail It's all right, the battle's over. Everybody won.

Nabal is frightening his servants. Can you find four of them hiding in the picture?

Abigail's donkey has disappeared under its load of gifts.

Colour the dotted shapes to find it.

How many different kinds of food is it carrying?

W	I	N	T	R	L	L	I	G	E	F	T
E	S	A	B	I	G	A	I	L	S	O	E
A	B	I	G	S	A	B	A	L	D	O	M
P	E	A	C	K	I	A	N	R	E	D	P
O	E	M	P	Y	R	N	E	A	P	O	Y
N	A	A	B	A	L	P	D	A	V	I	E
S	P	E	C	E	M	D	W	I	N	E	K
I	N	T	E	E	L	L	I	G	V	I	N
F	A	S	T	F	I	G	R	O	U	A	O
T	B	E	A	P	O	N	S	W	I	N	D
S	G	R	O	U	C	H	P	E	A	C	K
T	N	E	G	I	L	L	E	T	N	I	S

WORDSEARCH

Find the following words in the grid: ABIGAIL, NABAL, GROUCH, TEMPER, DAVID, WEAPONS, PEACE, RISKY, INTELLIGENT, FOOD, WINE, GIFTS, DONKEY.

Week 3: Jesus washes his disciples' feet

Thinking about it

What's the point?

Status consciousness is often a cause of conflict – we feel our own standing is under threat. Jesus taught us that the truly important people are those who serve and care for others. Getting this perspective right would make it very difficult to attack one another.

Doing it

Prayer

Loving God,
thank you for bringing us together this morning.
Help us to learn to care more about each other's needs
and by doing so to show your love to one another.
Amen.

From the known to the unknown

Have the children ever been asked to help with something, and then been given a boring job they thought was beneath them? Sometimes it's easy to get angry if we think our true worth is not being recognised, and wars have started over less.

Tell the story: John 13:3-17

(See page 82 for a dramatised version of this story.)

Smelly feet and toffee noses

Can you imagine a world where there are no cars or buses, so you have to walk everywhere? And it gets worse: trainers haven't been invented, and everyone just wears open sandals – and there are no proper roads or footpaths, so you get dust and mud all over your feet, and the grit gets between your toes and makes them sore. I tell you, the term 'smelly feet' takes on a whole new meaning in a world like that.

Well, that's the world Jesus and his friends lived in. So they had a custom that people always kept clean water ready for guests to use – and if they had servants it was they who got the job of washing guests' feet. Everyone knew it was a horrible job, so most people were too proud to do it if they didn't have to. 'I wouldn't be seen dead washing someone's feet,' they used to say – which of course they wouldn't. Who would? It would make a great headline, though, wouldn't it – 'DEAD BODY OPENS FOOT-WASHING SALON' – I don't think so. Anyway – the point is it wasn't a job that someone with a social position to uphold would do.

Jesus did, though. He was having his last meal with his disciples, and he knew they still hadn't really learned his way of thinking. So he got up from the table, stripped to the waist and went and fetched a bowl of water and a towel.

'Hey,' Andrew said, 'What's going on? Why's the boss doing this job?'

'I don't know,' James answered. 'No sense of his own dignity, that's Jesus' trouble.'

Jesus ignored them and carried on – kneeling at their feet and bending over them as he lovingly removed every bit of mud and grit, and dried their feet with his towel.

Peter was getting more and more anxious. 'I can't have this,' he thought. 'I have to look up to Jesus – if I can't look up to him, what does that make me?' And as he watched Jesus kneeling there, shuffling from feet to feet on his knees, he began to feel more and more embarrassed. When Jesus got to him, he couldn't contain himself.

'Hey, Jesus – no!' he said. 'You are not the slave around here. You are the boss – the Big Cheese – He Who Must Be Obeyed. You do not wash feet. And you most definitely do not wash *my* feet.'

Jesus looked up at him. 'OK, if that's how you want it,' he said. 'But if you won't let me do this, then it's obvious you want me to be something I can't be – so I don't see how you can have any part in what I'm doing, really. Still, it's your decision.'

Well, Peter *thought* he was the strong one – solid as a rock, you might say – but in fact he could change faster than a politician with a bad poll rating when it suited him. 'Oh, well, why didn't you say so!' he said. 'In that case, you'd better not stop at my feet. There's my hands, my head – why not tip the bowl over me while you're at it?'

Jesus looked patient. 'No need to go OTT, Peter,' he said, gently. 'Just your feet will do,' and he bent down to wash and dry Peter's feet. Then he got up, put his shirt back on and sat down again.

'D'you know what I've just done?' he asked. 'You call me the Boss, right? The Big Cheese – the Top Dog. I don't mind if you make me sound like something from a fast food outlet, but you need to understand this: if I, whom you think of as the big shot around here, have just washed your feet, then perhaps you shouldn't be too proud to do it for one another – unless of course you think you're greater than I am. This is what it's about in our community – we serve each other, and no one's too proud to do anything. Do you understand?'

'Sure do,' answered James. 'Does that mean it's your turn to wash up?'

Respond to the story

Discussion

Who do the children think would normally have done jobs like washing guests' feet?

- The head of the household?

- The lowest-ranking servant?

So, what is Jesus trying to tell us by doing this?

- That washing feet is a top job?
- That we should be less concerned with status and more with each other?

Song

One or more of the following songs might be used here and/or in the all-age worship:

Brother, sister, let me serve you
Let love be real
Let us talents and tongues employ
The world is full of smelly feet

Art and craft

✔ Have a selection of shoe-shining equipment (you may need to launch an appeal in advance) and show the children how to shine shoes. (See 'Word and action' in the all-age worship for how this idea would be used.) Have a few adult volunteers standing by in readiness for the service (perhaps they'd rather not wear their best trousers or expensive tights on that day . . . Also, ensure that at least some of the children will be wearing 'shin-able' shoes at the service – not all in trainers, etc. You might like to prepare a big sign saying something like, 'Shoe Shine Sunday' to place on the wall over the seats where the shoe-shining will take place.

Draw or paint a picture of Jesus washing his disciples' feet.

This is the key picture, but you might want to do others in addition to it, such as:

- The disciples enjoying their supper
- Jesus as the top man

Drama

See the next page for a dramatised version of the story.

Drama: Smelly feet and toffee noses

Narrator 1 Can you imagine a world with no cars or buses, so you have to walk everywhere?

Narrator 2 And it gets worse: trainers haven't been invented, and everyone just wears open sandals – and there are no proper roads or footpaths, so you get dust and mud all over your feet, and the grit gets between your toes and makes them sore. I tell you, the term 'smelly feet' takes on a whole new meaning in a world like that.

Narrator 1 Well, that's the world Jesus and his friends lived in. So they had a custom that people always kept clean water ready for guests to use – and if they had servants it was they who got the job of washing guests' feet.

Narrator 2 Everyone knew it was a horrible job, so most people were too proud to do it if they didn't have to.

James I wouldn't be seen dead washing someone's feet.

Narrator 1 Of course you wouldn't. Who would? It would make a great headline, though, wouldn't it – 'DEAD BODY OPENS FOOT-WASHING SALON' – I don't think so. Anyway – the point is it wasn't a job that someone with a social position to uphold would do.

Narrator 2 Jesus did, though. He was having his last meal with his disciples, and he knew they still hadn't really learned his way of thinking. So he got up from the table, stripped to the waist and went and fetched a bowl of water and a towel. Andrew was horrified.

Andrew Hey, what's going on, James? Why's the boss doing this job?

James I don't know. No sense of his own dignity, that's Jesus' trouble.

Narrator 1 Jesus ignored them and carried on – kneeling at their feet and bending over them as he lovingly removed every bit of mud and grit, and dried their feet with his towel. Peter was getting more and more anxious.

Peter I can't have this. I have to look up to Jesus – if I can't look up to him, what does that make me?

Narrator 2 As he watched Jesus kneeling there, shuffling from feet to feet on his knees, Peter began to feel more and more embarrassed. When Jesus got to him, he couldn't contain himself.

Peter Hey, Jesus – no! You are not the slave around here. You are the boss – the Big Cheese – He Who Must Be Obeyed. You do not wash feet. And you most definitely do not wash *my* feet.

Jesus OK, if that's how you want it. But if you won't let me do this, then it's obvious you want me to be something I can't be – so I don't see how you can have any part in what I'm doing, really. Still, it's your decision.

Narrator 1 Well, Peter *thought* he was the strong one – solid as a rock, you might say – but in fact he could change faster than a politician with a bad poll rating when it suited him.

Peter Oh, well, why didn't you say so! In that case, you'd better not stop at my feet. There's my hands, my head – why not tip the bowl over me while you're at it?

Jesus No need to go OTT, Peter. Just your feet will do.

Narrator And Jesus bent down to wash and dry Peter's feet. Then he got up, put his shirt back on and sat down again.

Jesus D'you know what I've just done? You call me the Boss, right? The Big Cheese – the Top Dog. I don't mind if you make me sound like something from a fast food outlet, but you need to understand this: if I, whom you think of as the big shot around here, have just washed your feet, then perhaps you shouldn't be too proud to do it for one another – unless of course you think you're greater than I am. This is what it's about in our community – we serve each other, and no one's too proud to do anything. Do you understand?

James Sure do. Does that mean it's your turn to wash up?

Jesus has lost the soap. Can you work out what's happened to it?

Pair up the shoes with the feet.

WORDSEARCH

Find the following words in the grid:
BIG CHEESE, JESUS, PETER, SERVANT, FOOT WASHING, MUTUAL, KNEELING, PEDICURE.

B	I	O	C	H	E	E	S	O	O	T	C
M	U	T	U	A	S	E	R	V	A	N	H
U	E	R	U	C	I	D	E	P	E	D	E
T	O	O	B	I	G	C	H	E	E	S	E
G	N	I	L	E	E	N	K	T	M	I	E
W	A	S	L	I	N	T	J	E	S	U	S
S	E	R	V	A	N	E	E	R	I	N	G
A	R	G	L	A	U	T	U	X	P	E	T
V	S	E	V	A	N	T	A	V	R	E	S
R	V	R	N	A	U	T	U	M	Z	R	T
E	E	D	I	C	U	R	E	M	F	E	S
S	F	O	O	T	W	A	S	H	I	N	G

Week 4: All-age worship

Opening song

A song praising and celebrating the faithfulness of God

Welcome and statement of the theme

Get one or more of the children to point out or hold up the pictures as you sum up the story:

Welcome to this all-age service for Remembrance Sunday. The theme, as we commemorate and honour those who have died in war, is, 'Make peace their memorial'. In Junior Church, we've been thinking about how we can truly honour those who have suffered in war, by actually contributing to a lasting peace, and we've been learning some lessons from the Bible. Firstly, we looked at the story of Cain and Abel – how Cain killed Abel because of religious pride. Then we went on to the story of David and Nabal. Remember Nabal, whose name meant 'Churlish'? Anyway, we saw Nabal's wife, Abigail, saving the day with some old-fashioned sweet-talking diplomacy and perhaps showing us a better approach to resolving differences. Then, finally, we took the story of Jesus washing his disciples' feet as an example of a whole attitude to one another that would make war unthinkable: service, not status, was to be the characteristic of his followers.

So, today, we're not only going to remember the past – we're going to try to learn from it and look to a better future. And the main focus today will be: [*Name the episode of your choice*]

Prayer

Loving God,
on this Remembrance Sunday,
we come to honour those who have died
to preserve the freedom we enjoy.
We want to honour them in the best way we possibly can –
by building the peace they died for.
Help us to learn to see other people not as rivals
but as brothers and sisters,
and ensure that the great sacrifice made by countless people
will not be in vain.
Amen.

Word and action

– use whichever is appropriate

From Week 1

Tell the congregation about the lucky dip, but emphasise that the game depends on complete honesty. If they like what they get, they can accept it graciously; if they don't want it, they must be honest and politely put it back into the tub. If they don't want to take part in the game at all, they must be equally honest.

Let the children go round the congregation with their tubs, offering them to members of the congregation. After a short time, when there have been a number of refusals as well as acceptances, draw the game to a close and call the children back to the front. Ask the people who refused how they felt about refusing. Were they embarrassed? Were they reluctant to offend the children? Were they afraid of seeming ungrateful? Did anyone actually accept something they didn't want, despite your injunction to the contrary? If so, you can assume a tone of mock severity and have a bit of fun.

Now ask the children how they felt when people refused. Did they feel it was a personal rejection? If anyone has owned up to accepting what they didn't want, did the child guess? If so, what did they think?

The point is simple. Rejecting the gift is not the same as rejecting the giver. Too often, we feel hurt because our work or our gifts are not appreciated – and we take it personally. That can lead to all kinds of trouble. It also applies on a national scale. More than one over-sensitive politician has felt personally rejected and uttered the infamous words, 'This means war!'

Now you're going to hear a story about this from the Bible.

From Week 2

Have the story read in either narrative or dramatised form, and then explain to the congregation that they are going to imagine they are under threat from each other and need to defend their personal space. Have the coshes given out – assure the congregation they aren't going to have to use them! If there aren't enough, others will have to improvise – handbags, hymn books, service orders . . . – until everyone has some kind of weapon in their hand.

Now adopt a quasi military posture and give them their instructions: 'On the command – wait for it, wait for it – join hands!'

Enjoy the resulting confusion, after which you can simply point out how difficult it is to hold hands and weapons at the same time. You could also say that the origin of the 'right hand of fellowship' was precisely that. In order to shake hands, people had to put down or sheathe their swords. Politicians are fond of the old maxim: 'To maintain peace, prepare for war', but that merely results in an uneasy stand-off. True peace is based on friendships – and as long as we're adopting defensive modes of being, friendships are going to be difficult.

From Week 3

In preparing for the service, ensure that there is a row of seats facing the congregation, where the shoe-shining can take place. Have the story read, in either narrative or dramatised form, and then announce that this is to be 'Shoe Shine Sunday'. The children are going to shine the shoes of some of the congregation. Although you have previously arranged for a few volunteers you may be willing to extend the offer to any others who want their shoes cleaned. Let the atmosphere be relaxed and informal – enjoy a bit of banter with the shiners and 'shinees' – 'I don't think I'd give up my day job, if I were you', etc.

Then turn the tables. The injunction is that we wash *each other's* feet. So those who have had their shoes polished now take up the kit and shine the children's shoes for them – kneeling humbly at their feet, of course, as they do so!

Silence

A time to remember, and to re-commit ourselves to peace.

Song 2

Offering

This may be introduced as symbolic or our recognition of how much has been sacrificed for us, and our willingness to offer whatever we may of ourselves for a more peaceful world.

Offertory prayer

Holy God,
we thank you for all you have sacrificed for us,
and today in particular all that others have given
that we might live in freedom.
In gratitude and penitence,
we offer you ourselves and our gifts,
that the true memorial of lasting peace
may be built in your world. Amen.

Song 3

Reading

Isaiah 2:2-5 read from a standard Bible. Introduce it with words such as: Isaiah makes a direct connection: learning God's ways means renouncing war.

Talk

Emphasise that this is not to demean the courage of those who have died in wars, and neither does it in any way detract from their honoured memory. On the contrary: to commit ourselves to seeking true peace is the best – the only – way truly to honour them and what they did. The emphasis in the reading is first on seeking to know God's ways and then, as a direct consequence of that, making war redundant. As Christians we must surely have the faith to believe it is possible!

Prayers of intercession

These could be led entirely by the minister or other adult(s), and/or could include some prayers written by the children themselves – or simply some points that they have raised in discussion. They should, of course, include prayers for peace and for the victims of war.

Song 4

Closing prayer/benediction